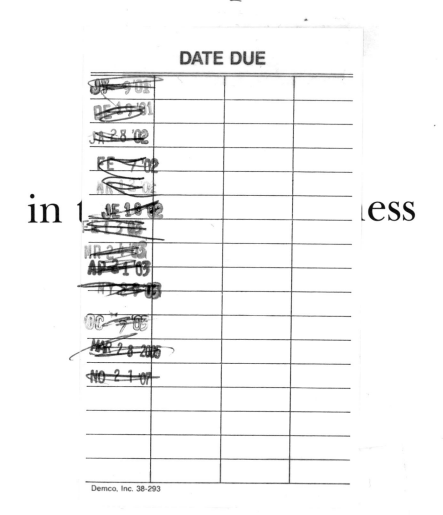
in t   ...   ess

Edited by Sally Englefried

6400 Hollis Street
Emeryville, CA 94608

©2000 Intertec Publishing Corporation

All Rights Reserved. No portion of the book may be reproduced, copied, transmitted or stored in any mechanical or electronic form without the written permission of the publisher.

Library of Congress Catalog Card Number: 99-62538

Cover Design: Linda Gough
Book Design and Layout: Linda Gough
Production Staff: Mike Lawson, publisher; Sally Englefried, editor

6400 Hollis Street, Suite 12
Emeryville, CA 94608
510-653-3307

Also from MixBooks
The AudioPro Home Recording Course, Volumes I, II and III
I Hate the Man Who Runs this Bar!
How to Make Money Scoring Soundtracks and Jingles
The Art of Mixing: A Visual Guide to Recording, Engineering, and Production
500 Songwriting Ideas (For Brave and Passionate People)
Music Publishing: The Real Road to Music Business Success, Rev. and Exp. 4th Ed.
How to Run a Recording Session
Mix Reference Disc, Deluxe Ed.
The Songwriters Guide to Collaboration, Rev. and Exp. 2nd Ed.
Critical Listening and Auditory Perception
Keyfax Omnibus Edition
Modular Digital Multitracks: The Power User's Guide
The Dictionary of Music Business Terms
Professional Microphone Techniques
Concert Sound
Sound for Picture
Music Producers
Live Sound Reinforcement

Also from EMBooks:
The Independent Working Musician
Making the Ultimate Demo
Tech Terms: A Practical Dictionary for Audio and Music Production
Making Music with Your Computer
Anatomy of a Home Studio
The EM Guide to the Roland VS-880

MixBooks is a property of Intertec Publishing Corporation
Printed in Auburn Hills, MI
ISBN 0-87288-727-8

Acknowledgments

Thank you: To all of the readers who have embraced and utilized this information. Here's hoping this updated, revised, and expanded volume will provide some added ammunition.

My sincere appreciation to Mike Lawson for his belief in this project, and to Mark Garvey, who first suggested I write this book.

To all of you who have attended, or will attend, my classes and workshops, especially my students at the Liverpool Institute for Performing Arts in Liverpool, England (LIPA), and the director of their Music Department, Arthur Bernstein.

Thanks to my colleagues—past, present and future—at the Los Angeles Songwriters Showcase (LASS), the National Academy of Songwriters (NAS), and *Music Connection*, *Film Music*, and *Grammy* magazines.

Thanks always to my family, friends, and Yuji for love, support, and inspiration.

Foreword

This book is intended as a guide for the professional and the aspirant in all levels of the music industry. It represents the expert opinion of the author but may not be applicable to all situations. The networking resource guide at the end of the book is current at the time of this writing, but because of the nature of musicians and organizations, some of this information may have changed.

Each reader will hopefully apply any material in this book to his or her own circumstances and will consult with legal and other appropriate professionals for advice as needed.

Contents

Concrete tips on making contacts from your hometown, creating a scene, and applying proven sales techniques to your networking efforts.

A final networking checklist.

A resource list of music industry events, organizations, and publications to get you on your way.

Introduction

If I woke up tomorrow, decided that my life's ambition was
to design sports cars, then picked up the phone to convey this
desire to the president of Toyota, I would most assuredly be
brushed off as a lunatic. Sports cars are designed by people
who have spent many years in design facilities and apprentice-
ships learning their craft. An outsider couldn't possibly break
into such an insular occupation with one phone call or hope
to achieve anything beyond the inevitable brush-off from an
icy receptionist and a subsequent hang-up.

Similarly, in the music business, telephone lines are clogged
on a daily basis by callers who are certain that they are, or
have, the "next big thing." Unwanted cartons of unlistened-to
cassette tapes and CDs are unceremoniously deposited in trash
receptacles, while the myth of the pot of gold at the end of the
rainbow continues to hypnotize yet another generation of
performers and songwriters. Unscrupulous companies prey
upon the unwary and uninformed, but the rainbow is an
illusion, the gold is painted on, and only the con artists profit
from the dreams of stardom and success.

In my career with the Los Angeles Songwriters Showcase
(LASS), the National Academy of Songwriters (NAS), and as
an independent publicist, PR consultant, journalist, editor,
and personal manager, I have observed thousands of people
desperately trying to break into the music game. As a 20-year
veteran of the music industry, I've been in a key position to
observe first-hand songwriters and performers breaking
through and selling millions of records. The latter possessed
the necessary skills, but they also directed their own success
through perseverance, people skills, and, above all, an
uncanny sense of networking.

Success in the music business is dependent on three key factors: who you know, what you know, and who knows you. Like any other business, it's a chessboard of players, hustlers, wanna-be's, used-to-be's, and someday-will-be's. In order to operate in this business, it is imperative that you understand who the key players are and what they do.

Almost no reputable record company will listen to an aspirant's tape unless it comes to them from a legitimate source with which they're familiar and, preferably, have done business with in the past. Even with these limitations on their accessibility they're still overloaded, yet new songwriters, artists, and performers are signed every year. How do they break through?

If you want national recognition, you have to create a buzz in New York, Nashville, or Los Angeles. If you want to stay on your home turf, you will have to play the exact same game. Like other businesses, the music business has respect for initiative and a quality commonly referred to as "chutzpah." This business, descended from rough and tumble 1950s New York, is not a place for the reticent or the timid. To succeed in it, you need a sense of finesse and a constant agenda of personal contacts and paybacks.

WHAT IS NETWORKING?

In the broadest sense, networking refers to any alliance, relationship, or communication with others in your field. This could be as simple as discussing with another musician what brand of guitar strings he uses when you encounter him at your local music store. When he invites you to his gig, or you invite him to yours, that's another step. When he refers you for a gig that he can't work because of a prior commitment is when the network begins to work on an economic level. Suppose your friend's band signs with a major manager, publisher, or record label. If you friend believes in your abilities, he is now in a key position to help you.

There is nothing new about networking; it's simply a new title given to ancient methodology. This book tells you how this methodology works specifically in the music business and gives you tricks of the trade and ways to increase your odds with specific plans and methods. It is a blueprint, as well as an explanation of how things really happen, and why.

1. **Every networking trick in the book won't help you if you don't have the goods.** The information included here can help you to open the doors, but once those doors are open you've got to have something amazing to shove inside. People who succeed as songwriters, performers, musicians, and technical and support staff are incredibly good. In Los Angeles, on any given night of the week, you can attend an "industry showcase" and hear unsigned acts and talent who are far superior to the top-charting artists of the day.

But are they as original as those artists, as visionary, as inspired? If you are a songwriter, your songs have to be better than what you hear on the radio, not just as good, because those songs have already been proven, recorded, and, most importantly, are making money for the writers and publishers.

This book will not help you write songs, play, sing, or perform better. However, if you already do these things well (or are on your way to proficiency), this book is designed to show you how to get maximum impact and to sell your abilities to those who can help you the most: your network.

2. **The most important ingredient for successful networking is being the kind of person that other people want to help succeed.** Your motives have to be positive, real, and honest— and so do you.

The first truth is fairly self-explanatory and is related to timing. If the time isn't right for what you're doing or promoting, all of your work and hard-won alliances can be for nothing. In the music business, you're only as hot as your current project. If you use networking techniques to get in the door and then have a mediocre product, you have no future credibility. Wait until you have the goods.

Work, improve, get feedback and opinions, but make sure you come in with full guns blazing. Your instincts are vitally important; and once you've used your personal networking contacts to give you a fair and unbiased opinion of your product, you will hopefully also have the judgment to know that the time is right to act.

The second truth is a little trickier. It's a business rule of thumb that in order to get something you have to give something of equal value. For someone just getting started in the business, this reciprocity can be tough, but think hard. Sometimes sharing in your singular sense of positivity and creativity can be all the payback others want or need. Naturalness and warmth are very appealing qualities, even to hardened music industry professionals. If people can help you to nurture your abilities, grow, and ultimately share in your success, they will be rewarded emotionally and financially.

Take a critical look at yourself in light of these two points. If you choose to ignore them, you will limit your chances for success.

MY MOTHER ALWAYS SAID, "LIFE IS TOO SHORT TO SPEND AROUND UNPLEASANT PEOPLE."

This particular platitude has the ring of truth. It's easy to grouse about the abysmal state of music at any given time; it's also easy to compare your lack of success to what is successful at the moment, but none of this does any good. You can sit around your living room discussing the negative merits of Madonna's latest release, but rest assured, she's not sitting around talking about you, is she? Don't say no with words, say yes with positive actions and an honest and full effort to get your music to where you, in your heart of hearts, know it must be. Don't let anyone tell you can't do this, either, because only you can determine how far you will go.

It's not just your positivity that will motivate others, it's the practice of the concept and being able to use that energy to make things happen. No magical person will emerge from the woodwork to wave a wand and make your career successful. This tired myth has to be debunked. Success in the music industry is a result of initiative, control, and craft combined with timing, understanding the business, having realistic expectations, and networking.

The current music market is very fragmented. Because there is a diversity of musical forms unheard of in past decades, there are more opportunities for musicians and bands that are out of the so-called "commercial mainstream." With the advent of affordable digital technology and the awesome power of the Internet, new opportunities now exist—but only for those who aren't afraid to take chances. In this book, we'll discuss how to call attention to what you're doing through self-determination and making your abilities, talents, and music clearly visible to your potential network.

WHAT YOU'RE GOING TO LEARN FROM THIS BOOK

I'm going to answer questions, debunk myths, and relate true examples of success through networking in the music business. My sources are some of the most respected names in the business. By understanding the alliances and career choices made by these successful individuals, you will be able to draw a correlation to your own circumstances, enabling you to take certain actions and make specific career choices. Because you never know when career- making opportunities will occur, a key to future success is to put yourself in a position that will allow career-making events to happen. You must learn to recognize and court valuable relationships.

EVERYBODY WINS

Songwriters need singers, singers need songwriters; both need demos, and studio owners need recorded examples of their studios. Performers need videos, and video companies need great-looking performers in the videos they show to future clients. Because everyone needs something, creative networking can allow you to create a situation wherein everyone wins. You can save thousands of dollars through systems of paybacks, barters, and trades. In this book, I will explore the options and show you how to trade your expertise in one field to achieve what you need in another.

Everyone loves a winner. Projects that appear to have backing and momentum will attract individuals hoping to benefit by association. Since many of these relationships can be beneficial to your project, it's important that you learn to make judgments about who can help you and to know when to court their favor.

Most major artists and trends in the music business over the last 40 years have sprung from specific "scenes," from New York's Tin Pan Alley in the 1950s to 1967's Haight-Ashbury in San Francisco to new wave on New York's Bowery in the 1970s to Seattle, Washington in the 1990s. Being part of a scene adds credibility to individual participants, and the media attention makes it all seem bigger than life. The press is much more inclined to write about music that also works on other more complex and newsworthy levels, whether it's political, social, fashion-oriented, or theatrical. In our media-driven society, pop music is certainly one of most talked about and written about forms of entertainment. For many bands, being a part of a scene has helped to thrust them into the limelight where they are then allowed to develop their own identity.

If you can't join a preexisting scene, the other option is to develop your own. In this book, you'll meet people who were canny enough to recognize and develop creative outlets for their talents and know how to actively involve other creative compatriots in their game plan.

Creative people suffer if they operate in a vacuum. Though our current technology allows communication through computers, e-mail, faxes, and machines—and it is digitally possible to simulate the sound of an entire orchestra in a closet—personal relationships have become even more vital. With the development of new technology comes the possibility of involving more people and their talents. Video has blurred the line between rock'n'roll and filmmaking. Corporate spon-sorships and commercial endorsements make the difference between a successful rock tour and one that loses money. Understanding the relationships between these various arts and businesses is vital to all entertainment people in this new millennium and beyond.

Musicians, songwriters, music business personnel, publishers, producers, students of recording arts, journalists, scenemakers, club owners, agents, managers, and anyone else currently involved with or hoping to be involved in the music business in any way will all need to know how to network successfully.

Personal relationships are the backbone of any business. In the music field, as volatile and shifting as it is, you're going to need some rocks to hold on to. These relationships, and the business you gain as a result of these contacts will help to anchor you and give you a variety of career options and outlets. It's a growth process; you won't be able to hold on to familiar places or people if you truly want to succeed. You'll have to change, meet, and know how to make the most of new contacts.

DO YOU HAVE WHAT IT TAKES TO MAKE IT IN THE BUSINESS?

Self-determination, initiative, and ambition are mighty tools indeed. The ability to adapt, grow, and educate yourself is of vital importance. Schools, classes, and books address these needs by supplying information to those who seek it. Music business aspirants, especially in the performing end, have a limited window of salability. The record charts are now dominated by performers in their late teens and early 20s, and they're getting younger and younger. Legendary rock bands ride on waves of popularity established at a much younger age. The application of the principals in this book will help you to maximize your moves within in a shorter period of time than you would otherwise.

Creating a public persona while working to achieve success is a necessity in an image-conscious industry. Nowhere else do appearances matter so much as in the music business; a personal sense of style is mandatory to create a favorable impression in others, to add to your recognizability and to make you memorable. In conventional business, men wear conservative suits, white shirts, and ties; in the record business, a person hoping to operate in the creative arena dressed in this attire would create instant distrust if not dislike. This book discusses these personal visual matters, analyzes them, and offers specific options. It is said that you never get a second chance to make a good first impression. The information in this book will show you how to make the best possible impression on the people who can make and break careers.

E-mail, letters, faxes, and especially telephone conversations are the jungle drums of the music industry. When communicating with your network of sources and contacts, information has to be conveyed in a concise and strategic manner. Many of the skills required for communication are also sales techniques that are necessary to convince others to buy your products, concepts and plans. In this book, we'll explore the differences between advertising, public relations, publicity, and promotion, and fundamental how-to's in each of these areas.

Networking in the Music Business is not just geared to readers in the music capitals. Many of the most exciting trends in recent years in the industry have come from nontraditional music cities. With decentralization comes an opportunity for performers and musicians to succeed without having to uproot themselves to go to New York, Nashville, or L.A. The same principals of networking will adapt themselves perfectly to the local level.

The music business is a traditionally male-dominated field, and women in the record business have often been relegated to publicity and secretarial services. In recent years, however, women have begun to make inroads in other areas, specifically publishing, management, and A&R. You'll see how the role of women is changing and how other minorities, especially Latinos and Asians, may be able to parlay emerging multi-cultural trends into lasting success in the music business.

PUTTING IT ALL TOGETHER

Networking in the Music Business is not for dreamers. It is intended as a working guide for anyone who is planning to make an impact in the music business. It is not just hard to break in, it is impossible without specific tools and information. This book delivers not only a concise and current insider's view, but also career and motivational blueprints, as well as eye-opening dialogue with key movers and shakers who have literally changed the face of popular music in our culture.

As you open this book, keep in mind that there is no easy way to succeed. The music business is one of the most, if not *the* most, competitive field in existence. It's also one of the most exciting and volatile fields imaginable, and for those of us who live and breathe it, it's the most important thing there is.

Above all, though, it's important to remember that none of this would exist without the music itself. As the business end becomes more sophisticated, it's essential that the music that motivates and drives it remains fresh, young, and spontaneous. The music should never be determined and directed by those only looking at the bottom line. The music business is one of the places where the true wild card can emerge, where an unheard of act can vault to the top of the charts, where an unknown can become a household word in a matter of months.

Behind these successes lies the most important element: the network.

What is Networking?

network is a group of people who provide the framework within which you do business. Networking refers to any contact within that interpersonal framework. In the music business your networking contacts will include producers, musicians, music store retailers, video producers, record and publishing company personnel, talent buyers, club owners, members of the press, and a seemingly inexhaustible list of fellow songwriters, musicians, and technicians. It's through networking that all business is done—not only music business, but every feasible configuration of commerce.

In the introduction, I told you that success in the music business is determined by three factors. Let's take a closer look at those factors.

- **Who you know.** Is your uncle the president of a record company? Congratulations, you already have someone to listen to your tape. But the rest of us will have to seek out and meet individuals down the long road who can help us get where we're going. Equally important, we have to be able to help them get where they want to go, too.

- **What you know.** You wouldn't be holding this book right now unless you had a desire to succeed in the music business, so you already you have an advantage. It's not just that you're reading this book, but you're a person with a quest for knowledge and the desire to fill in the gaps about your chosen profession. Throughout this book, I'll suggest ways to for you to educate yourself about the business. Many of these methods are inexpensive or virtually free. You don't need a ton of money to be successful in the music business, but knowledge is power.

- **Who knows you.** High-priced entertainers can afford to have publicists working for them full-time, but in the real scheme of things a fledgling music industry professional has to wear a number of hats, not the least of which is that of the self-promoter. You are your own best representative, and knowing where to go, who to talk to, how to present yourself, and how to follow up is crucial.

When your car breaks down, do you thumb through the yellow pages and pick out an unknown mechanic at random? Probably not, because when it comes time to make major purchases you don't always necessarily go for the best deal. Often you contact someone you know or who has been referred to you. Similar choices get made in the music business. It's not the best music that gets recorded, it's the music that has managed to slip down a well-established pipeline through definable commercial channels to reach a targeted audience of buyers.

Unless you have contacts, your music will never be heard by anyone. You can't hide your light under a bushel, you have to expand and meet others; hence, you have to build a network.

HOW DO I KNOW THIS IS TRUE?

When I was coming up as a songwriter, I wrote hundreds of songs in different styles, and I even had a staff writing deal in Nashville at one point. But it wasn't until I began working with a cowriter who had major contacts did any of my songs get recorded and begin to generate income. The songs that made money were not, by any stretch of the imagination, the strongest songs from an artistic standpoint. However, they were for specific artists that we knew needed songs at that moment (*timing*), who needed the specific style of songs we had (*suitability*), and who we could get to (*networking*). One of the songs was recorded by an aging pop/jazz legend; we played the song over the phone for her *hairdresser*, who loved it. We overnighted a tape and lyric sheet from New York to Los Angeles, and the next day, lo and behold, we had a commitment from her to record the song.

That's a true story; here's another. I met a publisher at a song-writer conference. He had contacts at ABC-TV who required a song about "getting rich quick" He told the network that he had a perfect song, then proceeded to stall them for a couple of hours. In four hours, a cowriter and I not only wrote a song, but created an atmospheric demo for the show. When the publisher turned it in to the show's music producer he "loved the Randy Newman feel." The song aired on *General Hospital* repeatedly for about a month, accruing valuable airplay monies for all parties involved.

Doing the job and getting the job are very separate functions, so let's face it, it's not the best songs, the best acts, or the best music that gets over, it's the most connected. Rather than mourning this simple fact, get on with it—network. Align yourself with others who are success-oriented and can help you create and market salable product.

I'VE GOT A GREAT SONG FOR WHITNEY HOUSTON!!!

Through working in administrative positions at songwriter organizations, I've met about a zillion songwriters. I love writers, neurotic creatures that they are (I of course include myself in that category!)—but sometimes the novice writers' expectations for their songs are so unreasonable that they border on the bizarre. I've met writers who played me of one of their songs and claimed that if they could "...only get it to (*insert one*) Mariah Carey, Garth Brooks, Madonna, Brandy, etc.," the artist would love it, cut it, and life would be a beautiful dream of milk 'n' honey.

So, you've got a great song for Whitney Houston. My plumber probably has a great song for her too, but the truth of the matter is that Whitney is surrounded by successful people, has access to the best writers in the business, and works with monumental writer/producers who have songs for her too. All of the songwriters who have already written chart hits for her have stuff too, plus access and credibility, so where does that leave you? It's astounding to me how many novices in the music business spend their time and money trying to access the names addresses and phone numbers of artists' managers and sending tapes and letters that go directly in the circular file.

Would you get very excited about a no-name singer with a development deal who was doing a one-shot at a smoky club singing Broadway show tunes? This is exactly what Whitney Houston was doing back when Arista Records brought her to Los Angeles to have her perform at an industry showcase. They invited all the heaviest songwriters in town, many of whom didn't bother to show up. Whitney sang her heart out and the rest is, as they say, history.

Once people become successful they have so many middle-people creating barriers between them and the world that their existence is isolated and unreal. The demands on their time are intense, and access to them is very limited.

The lesson here is to get in on the ground floor and meet artists when their careers are beginning. Be a part of the nurturing and development phase, make yourself an integral part of what they're doing, and expend your valuable energies on the creation of a mutually beneficial relationship.

Instead of craning your neck staring at the stars, begin to look around you at people you may already know or situations that you can control. Control is one of the most valued commodities in the music business. When you're beginning your career you may not earn any money from your endeavors, but you do own everything you create. As you begin to advance your career, elements of your creations will be reassigned—a publisher will own pieces of your publishing rights, a record companies will own the right to market your music, merchandising companies will own the right to market your likeness. You'll pay a manager somewhere between 15 and 20 percent of your earnings, an agent 10 percent of your booking fee, a business manager and a music business lawyer up to 5 percent each of your advance funds from the record company.

At the onset of your career, it's important to have a grasp of the fundamental elements that make up a career, to have strong goals, and to understand that, ultimately, you'll direct more of your destiny if you're educated and have a strong, positive network of people you can depend on.

LINKED CIRCLES

Your network is more than just a single group of people. There are many interconnected networks. After a recent concert, I held a reception for my management client. In observing the interaction of the band, musicians, technicians, journalists, and assorted party-goers and scenemakers, I saw that the specific networks resembled rings, circles of contacts that were interwoven and connected, as shown in the illustration on the following page.

All the divergent groups in one physical place are linked through their relationship to the primary event. Therefore, each individual member of each network has an opportunity to move freely between interconnecting networks, or circles.

At my reception, the *artist* was obviously the focal point of the event, and works with management, the staff, and the musicians. Since the artist is signed to a *record label*, the A&R department and the director of publicity were both in attendance. One of the musicians is from *Brazil* and invited his friends to the party. Some of his friends are also *technicians* and *studio owners*. The show used a troupe of *dancers* who invited their friends. We used this opportunity to premiere a video (with performances by the *artist, dancers,* and *musicians* and sound by a *technician* and *studio owner,* overseen by the *record company*), so the *video company* was also in attendance. All of this was being observed by the *press,* who were invited by the *artist* and the *management.*

We are all capable of putting ourselves in these kinds of situations. By limiting yourself to contacts within one small network, you are limiting your opportunities. The goal is to make new contacts constantly. Meeting new people and establishing new working relations is the key to a successful career.

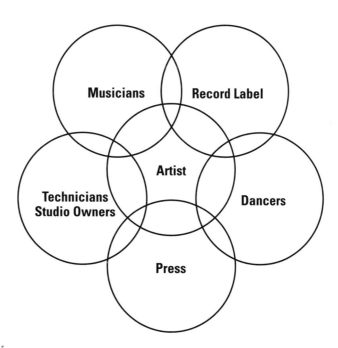

Music Biz Myth #1: *All of this networking is OK for some people, but I'm an artist; I like to stay in my space and create.*

The Facts: Creating is wonderful, and most people certainly need privacy to do so. Creative people, though, often neglect the most essential elements of commercial enterprise: sales. Selling doesn't have to be sleazy or deceptive; it's simply a new hat that you put on. Networking can be just as creative as writing or recording, but instead of working with a sound palette, you're working with interpersonal relationships.

The Modern Music Industry

UNDERSTANDING RELATIONSHIPS IN THE MUSIC BUSINESS

usic industry employees change jobs about as often as most of us change our clothes. It's a constantly shifting panorama in which many of the movers acquire the same or better positions at other companies within the industry. Thus, it is absolutely necessary that you read the weekly bible of the music industry, *Billboard* magazine, to educate yourself about the business, keep yourself current, and begin to understand trends and the economic climate. *Billboard* is expensive to subscribe to (although it is a legitimate business expense and therefore tax-deductible), but it is available at most libraries.

Now, let's consider some of the people you are ultimately aiming to reach as you network. Specifically, these include A&R reps, music publishers, producers, lawyers, musicians, and journalists.

A&R

If you're managing artists or if you're an artist or songwriter yourself, you will eventually need to deal with the record company's A&R (short for artist and repertoire) department. A&R is the ears of a record label. Employees in this division are typically young, energetic, and hard working. Often A&R people do not have the coveted signing power, but their endorsement of your music and their unwavering belief in your commercial potential can make the difference in your being signed or not.

A strong commitment and endorsement from A&R is a necessity for any act. Some established acts even have what is as a "key man" clause in their contract, stating that if their A&R person leaves the company, the act has the option of doing so also.

A rule to remember in dealing with A&R and record companies in general is this: *loyalty is to individuals not to companies.* To illustrate this point, imagine this scenario. An enthusiastic young A&R person convinces her label to sign a band she believes in very strongly. She nurtures the band, attends recording sessions, helps them choose songs, and acts as an unofficial den mother for the group. Unfortunately for the act, she is wooed away to another company with the promise of more money and power. The band is still at the original label but without a champion or any support from the A&R person's successor (who has her own acts to support). The band runs into budget trouble with their recording, and the label, rather than investing any more dollars in the project, refuses to allow them to finish their recording and puts it on the shelf. The band at this point has three options: (1) They can repay their advance and recording costs and buy back their contract. (2) If they can interest another label in their half-finished project, that label can possibly arrange a "buy-out" of the original contract from label number one. Of course, the band shouldn't expect any money in the form of an advance, since label number two is having to pay for what they've already done. (3) The band can wait out their contract, which may be a period of years and after which they'll be free to go elsewhere to sell themselves again.

However, not all these options may be available to the band. Keep in mind that in corporate America, it's not enough for your company to make money; the goal is to have the other company lose money. Therefore, for label one to allow the band to go to label two to generate economic gains for that company would violate this most basic rule of business. In this case, a record deal is not the end of the rainbow, it's the beginning of a long nightmare.

What Do A&R People Look For?

This is a subjective question, but the bottom line is that A&R reps look for *acts that touch them emotionally and that they know can make money for their companies.* An A&R person's job depends on his or her intuition, and many an A&R rep has joined the unemployment lines when a band stiffs. A band with a support network, a strong knowledgeable manager, a known attorney, a track record of live performances, a great demo, a strong independent release, and a video indicates that the band means business.

Music Biz Myth #2: *My songs are so good that even recorded on a $25 tape recorder with a hand-printed lyric sheet it's obvious I'm a genius.*

The Facts: I meet acts and songwriters with substandard demo tapes who assume that A&R reps have some remarkable vision that enables them to see beyond such shoddy submission materials. *In order to make yourself signable, you have to appear to be already signed.* Your recordings have to be first rate. Your CDs and lyric sheets have to look totally professional, just like commercial recordings do. Press and bio materials have to be on a level that the label representative is used to seeing and comparable to what their companies generate in their publicity departments. The less work an A&R rep has to do to get your act up to signing level, the easier it is to sign you.

To be deemed ready to be signed by a major label, you usually have to have a track record locally or regionally, you've got to come in with a manager or a producer whose credibility is so strong that the label will sign you on the basis of your support team, or you've got to be so fresh and unique that your sala-bility is undeniable. If you don't fulfill at least one of these requirements, you're probably not ready for the big leagues yet. But take heart, no one starts at the top and, as the ancient Chinese philosopher said, "The journey of a thousand miles begins with a single step."

I attended a music business symposium recently where a participant on a panel was asked, "How does my act meet A&R people?" The A&R person responded, "Create a buzz, play out, generate press, reviews, and an audience, and we'll find you."

With the remarkable advent of the Internet, the role of the record company is the throes of dramatic change. The CD format is allegedly on its way out to be replaced by mini-discs (popular in Japan) and an even more compact technology of credit card-sized receptacles that are capable of holding compressed MP3 files that have been downloaded over the Internet.

In many regards, the Internet has leveled the playing field, allowing independent bands the exact same presence as the majors. But listeners still have to find sites via search engines, hear the music, and want to purchase the product. Record companies possess distribution power: the ability to put product anywhere they deem it profitable, especially retail outlets. Today, it is not at all uncommon to see records being sold through "alternative marketing" including coffeehouses, gift shops, and other retail concerns.

But it is still record stores, either chains or what are commonly referred to as "Mom & Pops" (smaller, independent stores), where buyers go to find music. It is estimated that over 60 percent of record store purchases are unplanned. This means that consumers are inspired to buy according to what they see in retail stores in light boxes, posters, positioning, or "end caps" (product placed at the ends of the rows). In-store play is another huge factor, as are listening posts, where listeners may hear new releases.

All of these sales devices have prices. Space in a retail record store—whether at the end of the row, on a listening post, or in a light box or poster on the wall—has been paid for. Multiply one store times the thousands across the country, and the economics are overwhelming. A large record company can pay the piper on the retail level. Whether the format is CD, mini-disc, or downloadable files that will be sold from kiosks or off the Internet directly, the record labels will be there to handle distribution.

Niche Marketing: Do You Fit In?

While lecturing at a class at UCLA Extension in Los Angeles, I met a young man named David Yakobian. A musician/ producer/songwriter and performer, David, with contagious enthusiasm, shared his concept for Jewish Party Music. The formula was this: he would take traditional Jewish songs (all with copyrights in the public domain) arrange them with high-energy modern tracks, and market them directly to consumers. He enlisted me to write his ad copy—to which I contributed the tag line "even the Goyim enjoy 'em" (this is why I get the big bucks!).

When his first effort for his fledgling label sold over 65,000 copies, it was clear that David had tapped a lucrative niche. Since he was the owner of the company, he kept the lion's share of the profits which he in turn reinvested into recording Volumes II and III, making videos of Jewish Party Dances, and branching out into other CDs that all incorporated similar novel concepts. As of this writing, his label, Worldwide Success Records, is not only a name, but it's a self-fulfilling prophecy, with over 30 CDs in their catalog.

I once wrote an artist's bio for Joyce Handler, a classically trained musician and psychologist who was creating music for the purposes of healing first the psychic scars from her own childhood, then those of her patients. Over the next few years she wrote, recorded, and released a CD through her company, HealingArt. Today, Joyce enjoys a dual career as both a psychologist and a concert artist and travels across the United States lecturing at conferences and seminars performing a one-woman show, conducting workshops, and selling CDs. She has been very successful at sharing her vision with a growing, appreciative audience.

Neither David nor Joyce is an artist in the mainstream. However, for an artist on a major label to accrue the same income these performers earn would require literally millions of records to be sold. As independent artists following their own inspired paths, David and Joyce have blossomed and succeeded.

If you create original music and can define, target, and market to a specific audience, you may want to consider an independent route.

Music Publishers: The New A&R?

With labels tightening up in developing new acts, music publishers have moved in to take up some of the slack. Music publishers help songwriters find outlets for their material. For their efforts, music publishers take a percentage of income generated by airplay on radio and television and record sales (also referred to as mechanical royalties). In a business that counts pennies, millions of dollars are made this way annually.

Typically, songs are broken into two pies. A writer owns 100 percent of one pie, the "writer's share," and when he creates the work (if he has no cowriter), he also owns 100 percent of another pie, the "publisher's share." Signing with a publisher is a major step for a songwriter because the publisher's job is to find outlets for songs by having them commercially recorded and used for profit. For his efforts, a publisher is assigned a percentage—up to 100 percent—of the publisher's share. A writer with a track record often owns all or part of his publishing income; a new songwriter may assign much of the publisher's share to a specific company in return for an advance on eventual revenues.

In recent years, the trend has been for a publishing company to sign a band and give them money (which can be as little as $100 a week or up to about $500) in the form of a *recoupable* advance. The band can then make demos and, theoretically, live on the money they're given. They are "in the business," and they have a publisher actively seeking out career opportunities for them, including a record deal, and providing much needed creative and emotional support. Since many publishing companies are owned or affiliated with record labels, the possibility also exists of the band's being able to sign with a major label via that label's publishing arm.

All of this looks good on paper. The downside is that the publishing income from a hit song can amount to much more than what the publishing company has paid you in return for your publishing. To sign this type of deal, you should not only consult with knowledgeable legal consul, but you should also consider your own belief in the long-term financial viability of your work. The bright side to this arrangement is in knowing that a publisher can be a powerful ally. If career development for an artist is in order and you have the interest of a legitimate publisher, you have a distinct advantage. Many of the current deals for bands that write their own material are copublishing agreements in which the publisher administers the publishing and shares in a predetermined percentage of the 100 percent publisher's share. The writer then retains a piece of his publishing in addition to his percentage of the 100-percent writer's share pie.

For more on music publishing read *Music, Money, and Success* by Todd and Jeff Brabec (Shirmer) and *Music Publishing: A Songwriters Guide* by Randy Poe (Writer's Digest Books). You should also know that the bible for songwriters that incorporates everything you need to know is *The Craft and Business of Songwriting* by John Braheny (Writer's Digest).

Production Deals

Another way into the maze of this record world is through a production agreement. Explained simply, it works like this: an artist signs with a producer. The producer then records the artist and shops the finished product to the record label, which distributes and markets the product. The record label pays royalties to the producer, who then pays the artist. Depending on the clout of the producer and his track record, this method can work well to expose new, unusual artists who wouldn't otherwise have a shot. However, it can also chain artists to producers through control of their recordings, publishing rights to their songs, and management of their careers.

Both TLC, the Atlanta-based female group, and singer Toni Braxton made recent headlines with their familiar tales of woe: millions of records sold and not enough money to live on. This is an unfortunate tradition endemic to certain producer/artist relationships.

If you choose to work with a producer, always check out their reputation in the industry, make sure that the direction they want to take you in is compatible with your vision of your music, and make sure that you share a common vision. There is a legal term called *overreaching*. This is what happens when a producer or artist manager takes unfair advantage of a novice performer by controlling an unfair share of the recording, writing, or performing income. Trust your instincts, and avoid any situation that has this potential.

You should now have some idea of the people you need to ultimately reach in your network and the roles they play. Always contact a reputable music business attorney before signing anything.

CHANGES IN THE MUSIC BUSINESS

The music business, particularly the record business, works in cycles. Just because a certain label is not selling millions of units this year has nothing to do with what they may be capable of moving next year. In the last few years, with the awesome buying power of Edgar Bronfman's Seagram Corporation (which purchased MCA and owns the Universal Music Group), the record business has become even more of a giant conglomerate.

The record business is becoming more international. The U.S. market is shrinking, with roughly 33 percent of all records produced and marketed being sold in the U.S., while Europe (with Germany at the forefront) now accounts for almost 30 percent. The baby boomers, who grew up on rock'n'roll in the 1960s and '70s, can fill radio station coffers with advertising dollars, but they're less inclined to buy records than younger audiences. In Mexico and the rest of Latin America, the buying demographic is much younger than in the U.S., and in Europe acts that play clubs in the U.S. can often be seen in arenas. In Japan, superstar U.S. acts may also perform in arenas, but the record sales are strictly dominated by Japanese artists.

Author/theorist Marshall McCluhan wrote about the "global village," explaining that as certain parts of the world come together politically and ideologically, there is more opportunity for an open exchange of ideas, cultures, and music. Indeed, the breadth of music that makes up the pop mainstream in the U.S. is pretty amazing: hip-hop, country, Italian opera, trance, and melody-driven pop and R&B. The success of sampling breathes new life into old catalogs. The newest thing may well be derived from an ancient form.

The buyers are also increasingly fragmented. Dance, Latin (which has a multitude of subcategories), adult contemporary, alternative, and urban music all serve a specific group of buyers who, fortunately, allow for the economic survival of the individual purveyors of these diverse forms.

Country music in particular has made tremendous strides. The success of Garth Brooks and Shania Twain has been nothing short of phenomenal. One simple reason for this is that the aging baby boomers who no longer relate to rock music can still buy records. And if you take away the vocals and the steel guitars, the rhythm tracks of country records sound suspiciously like rock records. Also, country music is now purchased predominately by women who prefer less truck-drivin' and whiskey-drinkin' songs and more intelligent lyrics.

In the music business, timing is vital. Ever notice that whenever a new sound or trend comes out, it immediately spawns pale imitators? Pop music is constructed with building blocks of familiarity. Points of reference must be included in every form.

Imagine sitting in a record company office in the dark ages before rap, explaining to an A&R representative that you wanted to record a type of music that was a form of rhymed speaking over a sampled and synthesized beat with no singing, and that much of the music on the tracks was from preexistent sources and samples would have to be cleared (permission would have to be granted) by the original copyright holder. Think you'd get a record company advance? Rap found popularity on the street because it had a singular style and fashion and political and social statements with which the listeners could identify. By the time its original producers had made their lucrative distribution deals with the major labels, even white rappers had appropriated and diluted the style (much as they did decades before with "race" records), and you could hear the formerly "gangsta" music being used to sell soda pop on network television commercials.

Rock, in its purest form, is absolute outlaw music. Bands that incorporate a renegade stance are capable of massive record sales. From Elvis through the Rolling Stones to the Sex Pistols and Marilyn Manson, the power of rock has always been its incredible ability to polarize its listeners. It's a love it or hate it proposition. Nonmainstream forms of rock like heavy metal, thrash, punk, and rap succeed because their practitioners can mirror the specific resentments and rebellion of their buyers. From Bill Haley to Snoop Dog is a shorter leap than many urban sociologists can imagine.

Rock is the expression of a vital need, a noisy outlet, and an elemental outpouring. Those who can channel, recognize, and cultivate this essential key will continue to grow wealthy from its exploitation. Today's outlaw form is tomorrow's corn flakes commercial. As audiences become more deluged by images emanating from every form of media around them, they will require more and greater stimulation just to catch their attention. What was once only visible through smoky glass in a Times Square movie theater is now mainstream entertainment. Welcome to the new millennium.

New forms of global media and a new emphasis on social consciousness can be seen through organizations and events like Lilith Faire, Red Hot, LifeBeat, Amnesty International, and the Farm Aid Concerts. Rock, after decades of bloat and excess, is becoming relevant and political again. The bands and entertainers who participate in these events obviously have strong feelings; they also reach a tremendous potential audience.

Use this strategy on a local level to call attention to your music. Rock in the real world is a potent force; in Haiti, a song sparked a revolution. Music has the power to bring people together for political thought and change. To quote rock poet Patti Smith, "People have the power."

Music Business Myth #3: *The Japanese and the Germans control our records.*

The Facts: Sony Music, a Japanese concern, owns Columbia; a German company, BMG, or the Bertlesman Music Group, owns RCA. However, as with foreign ownership of the movie studios, the end product is not controlled by the parent companies; they simply control the bottom corporate line. The Japanese companies, which were very interested in entertainment-related commodities and acquired many of them during the last decade, are now struggling with the reality of their own country's struggling economy. The bottom line is: the music industry is a profit-oriented machine. The ownership is secondary to its primary function, which is to make money.

Music Biz Myth #4: *The music business is run by gangsters.*

The Facts: Organized crime has always been a factor in the distribution of goods and services having to do with the entertainment world. The music business is no exception to this, particularly in the realm of record promotion and wholesaling. Periodic payola scandals have rocked the industry since the late 1950s. When these are exposed, there is a great outcry and a subsequent purging of key figures; then, of course, business continues as usual.

The men who, a generation ago, formed the present-day music business were certainly not above doing everything within their power to assure the success of their acts. To a certain degree, it's exactly the same today. The music business goes by its own sliding sense of morality; a record company president can be fired from his position for phony expense account reporting from one company and be given the presidency of another company a week later. A chief organized crime figure can give potentially damaging testimony before a grand jury only to be welcomed back by them as an independent consultant.

With the corporate takeover of the record business, dealings will be under scrutiny by the corporate office and ultimately by the shareholders of stock in the company. The element of undercover players is certainly diminishing.

WOMEN IN THE MUSIC BUSINESS

The music business is notorious for being a male-dominated field. This has certainly always been so, but there are signs that maybe a few things are improving for women. Historically in the music business, women were relegated to the world of press and publicity. In recent years, more A&R people have been of the feminine gender, and as of this writing most of the major labels have women in A&R positions on their staffs, including as vice-presidents. Unfortunately, women have yet to make inroads into the highest echelons of the music business, the CEOs, presidents, and chairmen of the boards, with only two exceptions as of this writing (and that includes Madonna at Maverick Records). However, it's only a matter of time before intellect and resourcefulness win out, and more women break this barrier.

In the studio world, women have often been relegated to "talent" or to background vocalists. There are rare exceptions; some of the funkiest bass lines ever created on record were by Carol Kaye, a session bass player. Jennifer Batten, a Hollywood-based guitarist, can put 99 percent of the rock players in town to shame. In the world of record engineering and record production, though, the male domination is obvious.

Women in the music business are also subject to harassment, a situation that came to a head with the firings of high-level label personnel, one of whom was the president of a major label who treated his employees disrespectfully. I have a female friend who is currently on the road as a tour manager for a legendary R&B star, and she successfully fends off his amorous embraces on a nightly basis. For her to make a scene about this situation would be to risk her job, which she finds lucrative and rewarding.

As recording artists, however, women have dominated the charts in the past decade, including traditional artists and entrepreneurs like Missy Elliot, who has her own label imprint. Ani DiFranco is a fiercely independent acoustic artist who has resisted the majors and instead releases albums on her own label.

Even though women represent a small percentage of music industry executives, in many genres they are the largest buyers of records. Doesn't it make sense then that women in executive positions could determine what's a hit as well as a man?

MINORITIES IN THE MUSIC BUSINESS

The music business is a great equalizer in black/white relations. All of the great North American music forms, from jazz to rock'n'roll, have essentially been the grandchildren of African music. African-American innovators continue to provide many of the most innovative records to date, and the trends and fashions associated with these records influence every segment of our population.

Unfortunately, African-American musicians are often excluded from the rock'n'roll world and expected to perform only so-called black music forms. The imposed segregation from major label marketing departments is surprising, since music crosses all color lines. Black entrepreneurs, from Motown's Barry

Gordy to Puff Daddy, have used their influence to change the course of popular music. Chuck Berry and Little Richard, two of the fathers of rock'n'roll, were not R&B musicians but black rockers.

Though the pop world retains its strict black and white orientation, things have improved dramatically in the past ten years. True, only a handful of Latino rockers have broken through to pop stardom (like Richie Valens did in the late 1950s), but the emergence of Rock En Español is a potent force. In the rock world, the longevity of Carlos Santana and L.A.'s Los Lobos have inspired a new generation of Latino artists, and the breakout success of Latin pop music (though critics may argue that it's a homogenized form) has continued in a tradition begun decades earlier with bandleaders Xavier Cugat and Desi Arnaz.

Asians, with a fast growing population demographic, are only now beginning to be represented in pop and rock music by musicians and acts such as guitarist James Iha (Smashing Pumpkins), Cibo Matto, and a smattering of others. In most of the popular media encompassing film and television, Asians are allowed to be female seductresses, but the males are viewed as sexless mystics or glasses-wearing corporate nerds. This particular ethnocentricity is appallingly apparent in their nonappearance on the pop charts. Only on the New Age or classical charts do you generally see Asian surnames—which again, fits the stereotype of Asian as mystic or synthesizer tech head.

By uniting together to overcome the stacked odds, minorities have fertile opportunities to create new scenes, call attention to their music via sympathetic media, and make a difference. Pop music success stories will someday exist for all people. As stagnant as the music scene may seem, there is always something new on the horizon, and as we move into a new millennium, multiculturalism as a political, artistic, and social movement, is bound to influence pop music in North America.

HOW DO I FIND A JOB IN THE MUSIC BUSINESS?

You will rarely, if ever, see a record company position advertised in the "Help Wanted" section of a newspaper in New York, Los Angeles, or Nashville, because the number of aspirants wanting to fill these jobs greatly exceeds the positions.

Even though most record companies don't pay well, especially in the lower echelons, there is still so much magic and prestige involved that these positions are rapidly taken. Generally, interns are used at record companies, free bodies who do a variety of tasks. When paying positions open up, interns are often moved into them.

As record labels have been purchased and assimilated in the past years, many long-term employees have lost their jobs. If you need stability in your life, you should know that very few positions are long-lasting in this turbulent business.

Six Ways to Get a Job in the Record Business

1. Be an intern for a label.

2. Develop computer skills to enhance your employee potential.

3. Apply for a mailroom position.

4. Meet promotional representatives from the labels on the local and regional level who can provide a bridge to their companies.

5. Write articles about bands for magazines and newspapers in your area. You'll meet the publicity department and they'll soon have clips of your writing.

6. If you're optimistic, energetic, and great on the phone, apply to the publicity department. These jobs tend to have a high turnover rate.

In this chapter, I gave a brief overview of the current state of the music business and the people who operate within it. In the next chapter, you'll learn how to make contact with these decision-makers.

Meeting the Movers and Shakers

veryone currently working in the music business must rely on their own network of business associates to help them get their job done. In this chapter, we'll explore ways to contact those networks. We'll consider the networking opportunities in the three music centers (New York, Los Angeles, and Nashville), and we'll hear networking tips from some industry heavyweights.

ORGANIZATIONS AND EVENTS

Songwriter organizations exist in virtually every decent-sized city in this country. They are a fertile source to meet contacts —not only other songwriters, but also anyone connected with the business. If NARAS (National Association of Recording Arts and Sciences, the presenters of the Grammys) has an office in your region, by all means contact them. Musician unions, though not as powerful as they once were, are still a good source of contacts.

Volunteering for music-related events is a sure way to meet key people. Conventions and seminars typically require qualified office personnel, sound people, ticket takers, etc. to run smoothly. You can also work for free admission to these events. Working at philanthropic events enables you to do good works and meet good people.

It is also a distinct advantage to be involved in the organization of an event; this provides you with an opportunity to work with people with whom you wouldn't otherwise come in contact.

However, a word of caution: keep in mind that your primary responsibility is to the organization for which you're working. As an event producer, I can attest that nothing is more infuriating than a volunteer who is there only to make contacts and kiss up to the talent. I have been in the unfortunate position of relieving volunteers of their posts—even in the middle of productions—when it became obvious they were only there to further their own careers. Remember, effective networking is about opening doors, not trying to demolish them.

Retail musical equipment stores are frequently a barometer of the music community in a city. When I first moved to Los Angeles, within a week I was hanging out at a local store frequented by many of the top session players in town. By finding out who was whom, it became easy to meet some terrifically successful players and to begin to develop relationships that exist up to this day. Many times, employees of music stores are some of the most hip musicians around. They usually have a handle on the needs of the market and on who needs musicians at any given moment.

Music business classes at your local college can also be hotbeds of ambitious music people. Churches, especially if they have contemporary music, are good places to network in a comfortable and supportive environment. Alcoholics Anonymous (AA) is well-known in certain parts of Los Angeles as a great networking opportunity for musicians. In fact, I know people who have never had a drinking problem but attend meetings regularly in order to pick up contacts!

You need to meet people constantly in order to be successful in the music business. Look for every conceivable opportunity to make your presence known and to become part of your local music scene. It's important to maintain a sense of protocol in all situations where you'll meet industry people. Don't throw tapes in people's faces and don't be obnoxious. Do make an impression on them as someone they would consider doing business with. Act the part and act like you know what you're doing.

LONG DISTANCE OR LOCAL?

Without a doubt, it's easier to access the individuals who live where you live. Trying to establish long-distance relationships with individuals in positions in power, especially at record labels or publishing companies, can be very difficult. However, if you can make regular trips to the music capitols or attend conventions in major cities, these contacts can be parlayed into relationships. At some point in your life, you'll need to make a decision whether or not to relocate to a major music capitol.

Some people spend their whole lives regretting the decision they made to stay in their hometowns, while some people regret that they didn't. This is your personal decision, but in this book I'm emphasizing that a lot can be done locally. In fact, from an artist's perspective, it's many times much more advantageous to work in your own area, provided you can build up a substantial following and work effectively to establish your merchandising and recording base before contacting a record label. It is estimated that there are 10,000 rock'n'roll bands in Los Angeles. Want to make it 10,001? For more ideas on this, see the section in Chapter Five called "Selling Yourself from Your Hometown."

THE MUSIC CITIES

"Nashville, Tennessee, New York, and L.A. / Momma didn't raise her boy to run around this way."—DK

New York

New York is one of the most dynamic cities in the known world; its ferocious energy brings out both the best and the worst in people. The opportunities are many and varied. The theater world and the jingle industry offer many opportunities for composers, songwriters, singers, and actor/singers; the presence of world class universities including NYU and Columbia insures a constant influx of creative souls. The club scene is disappointing, though—except for the "showcase" clubs (read: pay-to-play) and some acoustic venues in venerable Greenwich Village, there usually isn't much going on. The jazz scene is good, however, and the rock'n'roll scene occasionally rises to prominence on the basis of some trend. For session musicians and jazz players, though, New York remains the big time.

On the livability scale, it's terribly expensive. As of this writing, even a decent studio apartment in a tolerable area may set you back $1250–$1500 a month. Recently, there have been massive strides to reconfigure what was once a crime-infested urban metropolis. It's still not recommended for the faint of heart, but I learned more about the way the real world functions by living in New York than I could have ever learned anywhere else. It's still the Big Apple.

If you go to New York, you can make use of the following organizations:

Songwriters Guild of America (SGA)
East Coast
1500 Harbor Blvd.
Weehawken, NJ 07097-6732
(201) 867-7603

American Society of Composers, Authors and Publishers (ASCAP)
One Lincoln Plaza
New York, NY 10023
(212) 621-6000
ASCAP sponsors a highly regarded workshop for songwriters engaged in writing for the theater. Call them for details.

BMI
320 West 57th St.
New York, NY 10019
(212) 586-2000

SESAC, Inc.
421 W. 54th St.
New York, NY 10019
(212) 586-3450

Study the *Village Voice* to find the names of clubs, see what types of music they use, and see when they hold open mic/audition nights. The *Voice* also has an extensive musicians wanted section, as well as ads for recording and rehearsal studios.

The Bleecker Street section of Greenwich Village has been a hotbed of musical activity since the 1950s, and it continues to be so today. The clubs on Bleecker, including the Back Fence and The Bitter End, are a great place to begin your search for a musical network in New York.

Nashville

For country musicians, Nashville is the best place to live. For musicians working in other forms, however, despite the presence of world-class musicians and studios, it can often seem provincial and limited. The live performance scene has expanded in recent years and clubs like the Bluebird Cafe do a great job of uniting the formidable songwriting community through one of the best live songwriter showcases in the country.

The transformation of country music over this last decade has been nothing short of spectacular. As the rhinestone-spangled drag of Porter Wagoner evolved into the dark intensity of Garth Brooks and Minnie Pearl's tacky hats gave way to Shania Twain's long legs, so did the sound of country music change in equally dramatic proportions.

Many of the best songwriters in the world live here. In the past decade, pop music has become increasingly limited for song-writers, since many of the artists (or their producers) write their own hits. In Nashville, it is still theoretically possible to pitch songs to artists who can take them to the top of the charts.

When I first moved to Nashville, I was told, "Spend ten years here and you'll be successful." I meet L.A.-based writers who return glowing from song-shopping trips to Nashville and raving about how nice and accessible everyone down there seems. After the glow wears off, they realize that, although they had a good time and everyone offered them that legendary Southern hospitality, they really didn't accomplish anything. Nashville is a very livable city with beautiful scenery, mild winters, and even an academic community, but if you're a northerner, a woman, Jewish, Buddhist, black, gay, or in any other way different from the norm of the tight white demo-graphics in this town, you may find it rough going.

A tip: Only tourists wear cowboy hats.

If you go to Nashville, you can make use of the following organizations:

ASCAP
2 Music Sq. W.
Nashville, TN 37203
(615) 742-5000

BMI
10 Music Sq. E.
Nashville, TN 37203
(615) 291-6700

Nashville Songwriters Association International (NSAI)
1701 West End Ave. 3rd Fl.,
Nashville, TN 37203
(615) 256-3354 or (800) 321-6008

Songwriters Guild of America (SGA)
1222 16th Ave. S. #25
Nashville, TN 37212
(615) 329-1782

Los Angeles

Los Angeles can be viewed as a blank canvas on which any picture of one's choosing can be painted. The historical capitol of movie-making, in the 1960s L.A. also moved into national prominence as a recording capitol. The opportunities are many in L.A. for songwriters, singers, and music business professionals. It is a very livable city with terrific weather, and the ocean, mountains, and desert nearby. You'll have to drive a lot! Los Angeles is also the capitol of the Pacific Rim, and the opportunities there have attracted people from virtually every country in the world, especially Asians and Latinos.

Los Angelenos are amazingly tolerant (although often self-centered), but smog and congestion are constant sources of aggravation. If you're properly motivated and career-oriented, L.A. can be great. The live music scene is constantly shifting. There are various scenes springing up all the time in various locales. L.A. is remarkable for the breadth of opportunities it presents for the creators of music, especially with the growing demand for music in film, television, video, and new media.

There is also a lively, growing theater scene as well as commercial production facilities and many recording studios.

The areas of Hollywood, West Hollywood, and the nearby San Fernando Valley (which includes Burbank, North Hollywood, and Studio City) are where most of the recording studios are located. The club scene is also in these areas, plus the beaches: Santa Monica, Venice, and Marina Del Rey. Silver Lake is a multicultural urban area where many artists and musicians live; it's also relatively inexpensive and very stimulating with many creative outlets.

ASCAP and BMI both present a variety of showcases for diverse styles of music. The songwriter scene also thrives on the "Caffeine Circuit"—intimate coffeehouses where songwriters perform, generally for free, tips, or just coffee. These are wonderful places to begin to expand your network.

It's essential to appear successful in this image-oriented environment, because the starving artist routine doesn't cut it here. Creative part-time jobs are plentiful.

Tip: Spend money on your car and hair, not your apartment. It's not just the city of the angels, it's the city of the angles.

If you come to Los Angeles, you can make use of these organizations:

Los Angeles Women in Music
P.O. Box 1817
Burbank, CA 91507
(213) 243-6440

This organization has been instrumental in developing programs for women's needs in the industry. They have a newsletter, hold seminars, and assist their members in finding out about job opportunities.

National Academy of Recording Arts & Sciences (NARAS)
3402 Pico Blvd.
Santa Monica, CA 90405
(310) 392-3777

NARAS presents educational forums for the music industry on a regular basis. They have full and associate memberships and have expanded their services for members.

Songwriters Guild of America (SGA)
6430 Sunset Blvd.
Los Angeles, CA 90028
(323) 462-1108

The Guild's popular "Ask-A-Pro" sessions can put you in instant contact with the music industry.

Pick up a copy of *Music Connection* magazine at any newsstand or 7-11 to get a feel for the musical climate of this town. *MC* also has the best free musician's classifieds going. The *L.A. Weekly* and *New Times*, both available free at music and record stores, cover all cultural events. They also provide club listings and classifieds.

Pick up *The Recyler*. Interspersed with free listings for everything from power boats to Chihuahua dogs, you'll also find "musicians wanted." Some of the most popular bands in Los Angeles have been assembled from these free listings.

CREATIVE READING

When you read trade publications such as the ones listed in the previous section, you should do so proactively. For example, if I saw an ad describing someone seeking musicians for a "world music/trance/Zydeco dance band," I might call the number in the ad just to see who has such a vision, even if I didn't need such a remarkable assembly at the moment. I've enlarged my personal network over the years by simply picking up the phone and responding to interesting ads, asking questions, and keeping track of musicians and performers for future projects.

CRUISING FOR A SCHMOOZING: TERRI MANDELL

One warm spring day, I walked through Hollywood to Crossroads of the World, a 1930s office complex designed to look like a cruise ship in port (only in Hollywood!), to meet with Terri Mandell, owner the Mulholland Group PR agency. For the last couple of years, Terri has been teaching a course on what she refers to as "Power Schmoozing." Schmoozing is an intense form of networking that takes place at gatherings, conventions, parties, and anywhere else that people come together en masse for the purpose of making networking contacts. Terri has lectured at conventions in Los Angeles and teaches classes regularly through a variety of educational outlets. The following conversation took place.

DK: If I walk into a room full of hitters, who am I going to talk to and what am I going to talk about?

TM: The first thing you have to do is get out of the hitter and nonhitter mentality, because most people have trouble talking to anyone. When you focus on, "I only want to talk to the person with the most expensive suit and the most expensive car at this party," it'll trip you every time, because that's when all of the fear and intimidation kicks in. So, the first thing you have to do is try to equalize everybody and practice on nonintimidating people.

What I teach is complete irreverence and rule-breaking. Here's an example: my friend and I went to the Key Arts Awards for the *Hollywood Reporter*—we went there to schmooze like crazy. So we're standing there and here's these three heavy hitters, Armani suits, ponytails, the whole thing, and my friend walked right up to them and said, "You guys look pretty important, you look like someone I should know, my name's Jim, who are you?" You need a sense of humor and irreverence—get all the pretension out of the way, be disarming.

Songwriters and music people have such an S&M mentality, but you don't want to come across like a nerd and stick your tape in someone's face; you can't be needy. Try to approach people as equals. In order to do it this way, you've got to have patience—give yourself a year and find ways to meet people through the back door. The front door is you call them, you send tapes, you leave messages with their secretaries. The back door is you hang around the places these people hang around in their nonindustry hours, such as fund-raising events for their children's schools, or you go to things like political gatherings and environmental groups, and you end up eating dinner beside this person. You're then viewed as a member of the in-crowd, not as some songwriter crawling on your knees up to him. Give yourself six to twelve months to build this plan. How can you go if you can't afford $500-a-plate dinners? You get involved with the group as a volunteer and you work your way in.

One secret about networking is this: you only have to meet as many people as possible, it doesn't even matter who they are. If you get that kind of momentum going in your life, the people you meet will lead you to others who'll lead you to others, etc.

If you, as a creative person, start doing interesting things, you create bridges for yourself. Create interesting activities—teach a class, write a book, don't be some guy who sits in his house and writes songs. A guy with a tape doesn't work. A guy with a tape who does organic gardening and is writing a book about motorcycle repair is something different. Make yourself more interesting.

DK: What should you wear? How should you look?
TM: My theory about that is you should stand out by not dressing in the uniform. For me, if I see a guy in a leather jacket, earrings, spiked hair, I know he's a musician; it doesn't impress me. I think somebody that dresses kind of grownup has a better effect. To combine the hip stuff with something kind of businesslike works better than the rock'n'roll costume, which just says you're playing the game.

DK: What attracts us to other people in a networking situation?
TM: Sometimes we're attracted to nonthreatening people, sometimes we're attracted to the most powerful person in the room; some people spend their whole night talking to the waiter. What pulls people in is a sense of humor, lightness, looseness. When you see someone who looks comfortable, it's real attractive, being verbal, being alive. The physical thing is very interesting—find the person you trust most in the world and ask for a critique of your physical presence. People don't know they have bad habits. If you ask a friend, a friend will tell you. Touching is real good—when you exit a conversation touch, shake hands, so they don't feel you're deserting them

DK: How do you tell if other people are ready to exit a conversation with you?
TM: They stop looking at you and start looking everywhere else. You know it's time to wrap it up. If it's you, the best way to escape is to be honest—don't worry about someone else's feelings, tell the truth. "You know it's been nice talking to you, I'm going to go on and work the room a little now," is better than, "I have to go to the bathroom" (because they might be waiting for you to return) or, "I see someone I know," or "I'm going to get a drink." Telling the truth is the only thing that

works. In a mingling situation, you'll spend about ten minutes with someone. You have ten minutes to make your presentation, and you've got to tell your whole story.

DK: What's a good opening line?
TM: People seem to think it's tacky to ask, "What do you do?"—that it's a pickup line or something. I don't believe that. Be real direct: "Who are you?" "Why are you here?" It's an OK thing to say. The only people who hate this question are the people who aren't doing anything. We have these notions of what's proper, and this is all wrong.

DK: How does it differ if you're approaching a group or two or three people?
TM: One of the rules we're taught as children is not to interrupt. In networking with groups, you're allowed to break in but only if it's three or more. If it's two people, there's a chance they're talking about something personal. You have to realize that a lot of events are for meeting people and not be embarrassed by that. You hover around groups, eavesdrop, and if you can hear something you relate to, throw in a comment—they'll either respond or not, then you move in on the group. It's uncomfortable, but march up to the group, wait till there's a lull and introduce yourself, casual as can be.

DK: How can you hone your verbal skills?
TM: There are these things I call everyday dress rehearsals. It's just like playing an instrument; practice having conversation with strangers on elevators. Talk to people at the car wash, in line at the bank. It's a normal thing to do, it's not a big deal, it's what people are supposed to do.

The following lists are part of Terri's class and are also included in her book *Power Schmoozing*. I gratefully acknowledge her generosity in allowing me to include them here.

Behaviors, Attitudes, and Styles
That Push People Away

- Smoking

- Drunkenness

- Sloppy appearance or bizarre fashion statement (acceptable in some circles)

- Hostile or depressed disposition

- Excessive profanity (acceptable in some circles)

- Bad jokes, especially sexist, racist, or lewd

- Talking too much

- Talking too little

- Too much hype and jive

- Bad manners

- Offensive smells (too much perfume, bad breath—ask your friends!)

Behaviors, Attitudes, and Styles That Draw People In

- A great but not overbearing sense of humor

- Good manners

- Confidence

- Nonthreatening appearance

- Smiling and eye contact

- Starting a conversation instead of waiting for someone else to do it

- Knowledge about the subjects at hand

- Knowing when to let go

- Not taking yourself too seriously

- Fearlessness

- Respect for cultural differences

Basic, Old-Fashioned (But Extremely Important!) Rules of Etiquette

- Don't interrupt

- Say please and thank you

- Don't be late (it's rarely fashionable)

- Always RSVP...on time

- Look into the eyes of the person you're talking to

Tips for Engaging People in Interesting Conversations

- Open by commenting on any shared reality you can find. Example: "Are you a member of this organization?" "Isn't this building beautiful?" "Can you believe the traffic out there?"

- Use multilayer sentences, and end with a question. Example: "No, but I'm interested in their work and I have a friend who's a member. She said it is a great group with good networking opportunities, so I though I'd check it out. How about you?" Contribute a lot to the conversation.

- Tell the truth. Example: "I'm a studio owner trying to expand my business, so I'm here to hopefully meet some new clients." "I'm newly separated and it's really lonely out there. I'm trying to meet as many people as I can."

- Have a sense of humor. Example: "I took a self-improvement seminar that gave us a homework assignment to meet three new people per month, and you're one of them!" It's a lot like telling the truth.

- Get to the point and tell everything. Example: **She:** My company is introducing a new soft drink aimed at affluent young singles. **He:** Really? You know, I worked on the ad campaign to Blarto Beer last year. I've done a lot of new product introductions in the beverage market.

- Create an opportunity for a second encounter. You don't have to close a deal on the spot, just create an onramp that you can complete later on in the party or on another day.

- Give the person something to remember you by. An interesting company name, a funny story that relates to something they're doing, a memorable business card, brochure, newspaper clipping, or other "take home" item.

"IN THE MUSIC BUSINESS YOUR DESIRE TO SUCCEED HAS TO BE GREATER THAN YOUR FEAR": ALLAN RICH

When I asked Allan Rich if he would like to share his experiences in this book, he was very receptive despite his demanding schedule as a writer. Allan has been in Los Angeles since 1980 and has written hits for top artists including 'N Sync, Whitney Houston, Barbra Streisand, Patti Labelle, Gladys Knight, Natalie Cole, and James Ingram. With cowriter Judd Friedman, Allan has been nominated for two Academy Awards, for "Run To You" from the $21 million-selling *Bodyguard* soundtrack by Whitney Houston and for "For The First Time," from the movie *One Fine Day*.

"I was working in Venice Beach, part-time, selling shoes. My friends who owned the store told me about a successful producer/writer, Howie Rice, who had bought ten pairs, and they said the next time that he came in they'd introduce me. He came in for the eleventh pair, and I was his salesman. I gave him a tape, and a couple of weeks later at 3:00 AM he called to say how much he liked the songs and to keep in touch. When I tried to reach him again it was impossible, so I figured, hmm, if he called me late at night he's probably a night owl, so I called him at midnight. I thought the worst that can happen is he'll be pissed off, but I can't reach him anyhow, so I may as well give a try—I don't have much to lose at this point. He answered the phone himself, and things started happening for me. If I hadn't gotten over my fear and made that call, my life would be very different today.

"I try to find a way to make people say yes, once they've already said no," Allan laughs, and gives this example. "I'd pitched four songs to Patti Labelle for her next album, and she'd put them on hold, so I respected that and didn't play them for anyone else. I was in England at dinner and someone at the table said, "Did you hear? Patti Labelle finished her album." I was devastated. When I went back to L.A., I wrote Patti a letter and let her know how disappointed I was that she'd held the songs, not recorded them, and hadn't communicated this to me. A couple of nights later the phone rings and it's Patti! She let me know that the record had gone overbudget, etc., but she still loved the tunes. We'd cut the demos in her key, so my cowriter Alan Roy Scott and I, being enterprising gentlemen, took the tracks to Patti's hometown, Philadelphia, bumped up to 24-track, and recorded her vocals. We used our own money, about $4,000, and they put the one of the songs on her album."

Nowadays, Allan's reputation allows him almost unlimited industry access, but as he explains, "It's still a screen test each time, it's still about rejection. You've got to put your ego on the back burner or, to quote Quincy Jones, 'Check your ego at the door.'" To young writers who would like to work with him, Allan says, "I got to write with Burt Bacharach, which was a thrill. My publisher (MCA Music) set it up. I met my collaborator Judd Friedman through his publisher at peermusic. She called me and said, 'We've just signed a new writer, he's never had a cut, but I think he's great, would you like to meet him?' The first song we wrote together was 'I Don't Have the Heart" [which went to #1 for James Ingram]. I have a hit list each year of cowriters I'd like to work with—maybe I'm on someone else's hit list."

Barry Manilow was one of Allan's first big time collaborators. The two met through Howie Rice, who was working on Manilow's album. Rich was asked to write a lyric to a melody they had, which he painstakingly labored over. "Then I go to Barry's house, which is a trip, because I'm still selling shoes at the beach. I walk in the house and find out that they've changed the whole melody, now the lyric won't work. So they send me home to rewrite. Barry is so jazzed by the melody that he's going to record the next day, but I've got a wedding that night, and the next day (Sunday) I've got to work selling shoes, which Barry knows about. So I go to the wedding, stay up till 3 AM, finish the lyric, slide it under Howie's door, and go to work. They call me later to come down to the studio after

Chapter Three   **35**

work, I get there, Barry comes out of the vocal booth and says, 'You wrote a good lyric, now teach me the bridge.'"

Another fortuitous job for Rich was as a waiter at the Source restaurant in Los Angeles, a health food music industry hangout. "I'd just start talking to people. I'd meet other writers, tell them what I did. I used to wait on Syreeta Wright. A couple of years later, I was in the studio and she was recording one of my songs. I said, 'Do you remember me?' She was amazed. I used to be her waiter, and here she was singing my songs.

"One key is to talk to and be friendly with everyone. You never know who you might be talking to who could change your life, so let everyone know what you do. Also, be sure to never write anyone off; the person you may be talking to today who you perceive as being nowhere could have a huge hit tomorrow, you just never know."

Allan Rich's personality is an interesting dichotomy, as well as a key to his success. On one hand, there's the persistent (but never pushy) networking, business-oriented songwriter. On the other hand there is a very warm, open, honest, vulnerable artist who believes that his greatest strength is in "being able to say something straight forward which touches people." Certainly, his hit songs all have this quality. He is also a tireless worker and someone who understands how the business works and who enjoys being part of the entire process. He is very involved in business decisions made by his publisher and, even though he is copublished by a major publishing company, Allan takes the initiative and responsibility for procuring his own cuts and charting his own course.

"You have to *make* it happen," Allan notes. He certainly does.

THE MUSIC BUSINESS LAWYER: DONALD PASSMAN

I am proud to have written one of the very first reviews of Donald S. Passman's book, *All You Need to Know about the Music Business*. When writing the review, I contacted the L.A.-based lawyer and invited him to speak at the annual Songwriter's Expo, which he did, eloquently, to a room packed with rapt listeners.

A soft-spoken, straight-talking, bespectacled Texas native, Passman's roster has included superstar clients like Quincy Jones, Don Henley, Janet Jackson, REM, and Lauryn Hill. He's negotiated some of the biggest record deals of all time. I met with Don in his office.

"I was around music all my life. My stepfather was a disc jockey, I played accordion in high school then I started playing guitar... When I was in college and law school I played in bands. When I started practicing law I actually made more money playing in bands, but I wanted to find a way to eat regular and be in the music business, so I decided to go into the business side. Now I play for my kid's campouts!

"After college, I came back to Los Angeles. I started out life as a tax lawyer, then I took a class at USC in the music business (which I now teach) and that was fun. So I changed jobs, went to this firm 20 years ago. It's still as fun as it was that first day.

"As it happened, this firm represented more firms than artists, so I was representing record companies, then I started doing artists. It was a gradual process to find clients. Our firm's philosophy has never been volume; we look for people we like and can develop a long-term relationship with. We keep it small.

"I have other clients who don't particularly look for commercial success; they want to be true to their art. I think with people like that, you get the deals that are consistent with who they are, you don't go out and try to maximize the dollars. You put them with a company who understands their vision.

"By the time I got in the business, my stepfather was out, so the only person I knew was (record producer) Snuff Garrett and a client of this office. In a sense, when I came here to work, I immediately got immersed in the business and there were relationships I could plug into. Aside from that, I made it a point to go out and meet people my age who were doing what I was doing. My theory was, as it's happened, that in 20 years they'd be in very important positions.

"Speaking specifically, I think that you should pick people who are doing what you want to be doing. You need to get around them to see how they do what they do. If you can't get to them, you can get to people who work for them. Remember, everybody was nobody at some point, no one had heard their name.

You want to get out and meet as many people as possible. Some of the people you may meet may be of little use to you (though they may be nice people!). You can make some friends, but you never know where some kind of a clue is going to come from. You've got to be aggressive about following up; you've got to be aggressive about chasing things that look promising. It's like fishing: most of the time you sit there with your hook in the water, every once in awhile you might pull one in, or shoes, or old tires, so you've got to invest what you've got the most of which is time. If you want to be an artist, you've got to be out in the clubs, not to copy but to see how it works, who is making it and why. You've got to study it like you'd study anything else. It's like if you were going to be a plumbing contractor, you'd go and watch the contractors—same thing in the music business. Read interviews, see how people got started, but remember, some of it's press hype. Look for names of people in the business, don't be shy about mailing things to people. It just takes time—set a reasonable time frame for yourself.

"The one trait I'd put on all the superstar clients I have is persistence. They're all very driven, very focused, they have a vision of who they are, what they want to be, how they'll get there, and they'll walk through walls to get to where they want to go. They'll pick themselves up if they fall down, walk around the barrier. And that's the quality that it takes, even more so than talent, it's persistence.

"Meet everybody you can, be nice to everyone because you haven't a clue, even someone who may not be a direct help for you may have information. It's not necessary to step on other people or to hurt other people in order to be successful. It's better karma if you don't, you'll last longer, have a happier life and sleep better. At the same time, being out there and being part of the group energy keeps you involved. Stay away from negative people, stay where the sun shines. The sleazes never ruled this business—they may have had a few artists they glommed onto early in their careers and sucked the life out of them for a period of time until the acts wised up and moved along with their lives. While there may have been guys who were aggressive or did things not everybody approved of, they never were never slimeballs—those were small players, because when you think that way you stay small.

"Everybody who goes into a new business does it without knowing everything. And a lot of people who grow up in the business are not successful. So it's not such an advantage to know everything about it—of course you do need a copy of *All You Need to Know About the Music Business*!! But you don't have to be well connected, just talented and persistent.

"It's possible to work on the regional or local level. If you're going to play in the big leagues, you're going to have to have representatives in L.A., New York, or Nashville. More and more managers are based out of other cities—it's not necessary to live here, but it's necessary to visit here to be in the business.

"The irony of this business is that people are always looking for talent. The perception is you can't get in the door and in some ways this is a reality. A record company can get five, six hundred tapes a week from unsigned bands, hopefuls, and most of the labels won't listen to them. On the other hand, everyone's looking for real talent, and if you're talented and good, you're going to make it in the business.

"USC classes, City of Hope, anything you can do and anywhere you can go to meet people and get your name out, is positive. The more you're around, the better off you are. If it's not your personality, hook up with a manager who's aggressive. You can have the best product in the world but if you can't get it out there no one will know."

MORE NETWORKING TIPS

When networking, you need to speak with everyone, everywhere, all of the time. When you're in a setting where you have direct access to people who share your aspirations and interests, give yourself every opportunity to be approachable.

In a networking situation, a sense of humor and honesty are your most valuable tools. It's up to you to dispel others' insecurity by taking an active role in engaging them in conversation. You will never go wrong by beginning with an honest compliment. Look your contact directly in the eyes, concentrate your energies on them, and be sure to smile. Ask general questions to keep them talking. For the period of time that you've engaged them, let them be your entire world.

Do:

- Ask, then remember, their name. Use it repeatedly in the conversation to burn it into your memory.

- Use open body language. Keep your arms and, if seated, your legs uncrossed.

- Be unerringly polite.

- Ask them what they do and why they happen to be there.

- Ask them for their business card.

- Use the environment around you to give you mutual topics of conversation.

- Sense when the conversation is coming to a logical conclusion.

- Keep the window open for future discussions.

- Let them know that you enjoyed speaking with them.

- If applicable, let them know that you'll give them a call.

Don't:

- Begin with a negative comment such as, "Isn't this paté awful?"

- Say, "Where do I know you from"?

- Give off a sexual vibe

- Talk about yourself continually

- Look over their shoulder and talk to people passing behind them (though it's OK to acknowledge others with a smile or wave)

- Forget their name

- Eat large hunks of food while speaking

- Say anything negative about any person present

Networking in the Music Business

- Pressure them in any way

- Act desperate

Make Them Remember You

A strong handshake, a well-modulated voice, an air of confidence, high energy, positivity, honesty, a sense of humor, and a unified visual appeal will make you recognizable.

When meeting people for the second or third time, don't assume that they know who you are. They'll appreciate it if you remind them, "Hi John, I'm Dan, we met last month at the BMI awards dinner." Generally, this is met with a favorable response—providing you made a favorable impression, of course.

Information about music industry personalities is fairly easy to come by if you know the right sources. If you were going to meet with an A&R executive wouldn't it help to know what type of music he likes, who he's signed to his label in the past, and his general likes and dislikes? Making others feel important is always a good approach. I've had success in knowing not only an industry mover's most recent successes, but also some esoteric piece of information. In addition to the magazines and periodicals that you should read regularly, train yourself to read the small print on CD insert booklets because the real truth often lies in the arranging and production credits, the thank you's, and the listings of the songwriters, publishers, studios, musicians, and management. Often there are addresses for management offices.

Collecting interviews with music industry execs is a way to access vital information. The biweekly LA-based magazine, *Music Connection*, provides an A&R profile in each issue of their publication. The information is invaluable for anyone in the business, particularly personal managers or artists hoping to be signed. Once a year *Music Connection* compiles this information into a special issue. You can contact them at (818) 755-0101, or write to: Music Connection Magazine, 4731 Laurel Canyon Blvd. North Hollywood, CA 91607. Check them out on the Web at www.musicconnection.com.

For a career in the music business, it's crucial to take stock of your assets and your liabilities. Since you're (hopefully) in this life to improve as a person as well as a music businessperson, you have to be honest with yourself and keep improving. Visualize your success, surround yourself with hardworking, honest, productive positive people, and success will be closer than you think.

We know that a network of people will be involved in determining our success. In order to cultivate these people and impress and influence them, you have to first meet them. Networking is far-reaching—through your contacts, you will meet their contacts and so on. Someone with whom you carry on a seemingly insignificant conversation at a cocktail party may well prove to be your most valuable ally in the distant future. You will never know the end results of your network until you've achieved success and can understand, with perfect hindsight, how you did it.

Therefore, you've got to work hard on being a decent, fun, and giving person. Talk to everyone everywhere. Cultivate your people skills because your charm and enthusiasm are invaluable tools of influence. No matter how talented you may be, if others don't enjoy being around you, working with you, and being a part of your network, you will not succeed.

In this chapter, you learned about the many networking opportunities that are open to all who care to apply, and you saw how some successful participants in the music business have established their careers through successful networking. In the next chapters, we'll examine you and your personal goals, needs, and aspirations. We'll take a look at what you have that can help you succeed, as well as what may be holding you back.

CHAPTER 4

What Have You Got?

SELF-DETERMINATION, INITIATIVE, AND AMBITION

was fortunate to have the opportunity to take a course in artist management at UCLA from one of the best teachers, Ken Kragen, who has guided the careers of Trisha Yearwood, Kenny Rogers, Gallagher, Travis Tritt, Lionel Ritchie, and Olivia Newton-John. A well-spoken, intelligent man, Kragen certainly dispels the unsavory image of the cigar chomping, back-room hustler. He has also organized two monumental charitable events, We Are The World and Hands Across America.

One of the first things Ken had our class do when we arrived at UCLA was to make two lists: the first was a list of things we most like to do, the second of things we least like to do. Initially, this exercise felt silly and sophomoric, but it gradually dawned on me what I was supposed to be learning from this exercise: how to find and establish a niche in the entertainment world based on these likes and dislikes.

Kragen taught tough self-determination. In the music business, you have to be your own boss and totally in control of your own destiny. For artists, believing that managers are employers who will tell you what to do and provide you money with which to do it is a ludicrous and erroneous assumption. Indeed, in Kragen's class there was a recording legend who had always been told what to do by her manager, but millions of record sales later she still needed to learn more about the business which had made her and her managers wealthy.

For the fledgling entrepreneur there is no pattern to follow in order to succeed. You must chart your own course.

LONG-TERM GOALS

It is imperative that you write down your long-term and short-term goals. Until you have set down this information in a form you can see, it will never be real to you.

Keep a notebook or folder with lists, goals, and objectives. No one else need ever see it. Your notebook will keep you on track and informed about where you need to be, what you should be doing, what's working for you, and what's not.

Your long-term goals should be everything you hope to do in the future. If you want to be rich and famous, fine, write it down. If you want to be bigger than Elvis, put that down. President of Warner Brothers Records? No problem, put that down, too. This list is for you—it's not for anyone else to look at, experience, or imagine. Dreams are wonderful things and allow us to see the big picture; goals are simply dreams with deadlines.

Determining your long-term goals can prove to be a daunting experience, because you must be absolutely truthful with yourself; there is no self-deception allowed. If you are a performer, you know what makes your audiences respond. Can you make an audience crazy? Will young girls and boys buy your records, put your picture on their walls, dream about you? Will they buy your records, videos, T-shirts, posters?

If you aspire to the business end of music, can you withstand the pressures involved in making million-dollar decisions? Can you look at the big picture and direct a team of people to do your bidding? Can you sit down with the president of a major record label for a power breakfast and not choke on your napkin? Do you look, talk, and act the part? Are you capable of managing, recognizing, channeling, developing, and ultimately controlling talent? Are you aggressive enough to go all the way for what you know you deserve?

What do you like to do? Do you need security, comfort, a home life that's relatively normal? There are positions in the music business that do allow for this type of serene existence, but they're certainly not the norm! The entertainment world in general runs on an amazing amount of energy, long hours, crazed conditions, and a phenomenal amount of travel. All these factors make for a harried existence. Job security is virtually nonexistent. Record companies employee salaries are shamelessly small, but so many people want these few available positions. To be in the music business, you're got to understand it's more than an occupation. It is more akin to a fever, one caught early in life. If you can change and adapt with the business, you will ultimately succeed.

You will find the answers to many important questions as you begin to develop in your career. You'll find these answers quickly, because the music business, like most of life, is not a spectator sport; you'll have to participate. "You either do it or you don't—trying doesn't count," says DreamWorks Records chief David Geffen.

HOW DO I DETERMINE WHAT I SHOULD FOCUS ON?

Determining whether to focus on being a performer, a writer, or a music business person is a crucial decision. In order to pursue your dreams, you must first define them. To recognize your strengths, first take a realistic look at your abilities:

Five Questions for Artists

1. Have you developed a recognizable musical style that is uniquely your own?

2. Are you more than a sum total of your musical influences?

3. Have you written songs that you can honestly say are better than what's on the radio? Have you found songs to sing that no one else can interpret with your feeling and style?

4. Are you being challenged by working with musicians who are better than you and from whom you can learn?

5. Are you spearheading your entire existence around the fulfillment of your musical vision?

Five Questions for Future Moguls

1. Can you recognize talent in others?

2. Do you have a distinct vision for developing talent?

3. Will others take you seriously as a business equal?

4. Can you see the big picture?

5. Are you spearheading your entire existence around the creation of a network that will help you fulfill your economic vision?

As you begin to focus on your most important goals, you'll have to decide which are attainable and why you deserve to attain them. Rock'n'roll heroes are people who have no alternative except to do what they do. Can you imagine Sheryl Crow as a bank teller? Bruce Springsteen selling insurance? If your career goals are more modest or focused on a becoming a supporting player, you may have better chance of fulfilling your aspirations. But if you take this path, you'll never be a rock star because to be one you absolutely have to be willing to put it all on the line, to sacrifice any type of a normal existence, to starve, to sleep on floors, to be treated like dirt for the fulfillment of your music. I don't claim this is exactly how it will happen to you but you do have to be ready to do whatever it takes.

I remember my father encouraging me to finish college so I'd have something to fall back on. I resisted this advice because of career opportunities, and I've never once regretted this decision. Know why? In my experience, people who have something to fall back on always fall back. In the competitive environment of the music business, you'll have no room to fall back. Never in my 20 years in the music business have I been asked if I have a college degree, although I lecture in England to college students at The Liverpool Institute for the Performing Arts and at UCLA in Los Angeles—and, of course, I write books, too.

Diversity is asset that can serve you well in attaining your goals. Although I began as a performer, I am now a manager, publicist, author, editor, and public relations consultant. Many people in positions at record companies play instruments and were drawn to their current vocations because of a love of music developed when performing in fledgling teenage rock-'n'roll bands.

Certain forms of destiny are out of our hands. Since this is not a book on religious science, I'll keep my observations earthbound, but one vital key is to always be open to new experiences. Don't be too close-minded to hear opportunity when it knocks.

I recently heard this sentiment expressed: "If things don't happen easily or naturally, sometimes they may not happen at all." At first this seems too simple—an assertion that may be taken as a rationalization. "It didn't happen easily, so I gave up," is certainly not an admirable stance for any hard-working music biz professional. But as I thought about it again, I began to understand an inherent truth: many of life's successes seem predestined. They just feel right.

When I made a career decision to shift my focus from writing songs to working on the other side of the desk, I was immediately met with an overwhelming sense of rightness and support. If, in your own professional quest, you find yourself trying to knock down walls, you may want to go around to another side of the house to see if perhaps there's a window open.

There are designated windows of opportunity in the music business. I recently interviewed an artist, newly signed to Capitol Records at age 17, who joked about "all the 40-year-old men" in her life. These included her producer, manager, A&R rep, and lawyer. Executives in their 40s are certainly not uncommon; indeed, that's a decade when many executives begin to attain very high levels of professional success.

Note that this was not a 40-year-old artist discussing all the 17-year-olds in her life. Young artists are the norm for record deals. Many times, older artists are deemed less flexible with a shorter career spans. All of their development has essentially been done. In pop music, this is a cold reality.

In many other creative areas—writing, painting, etc.—an older artist is deemed to have a richer, deeper understanding of their craft. But with the buying demographic patterns inherent in the music business, young artists are certainly the norm. However, note that this does not include songwriters, producers, managers, agents, executives, technicians, lawyers, publicists, musicians, tour managers, voice coaches, and any number of other highly necessary functionaries.

Personally, I would not be able to manage artists as effectively as I do had I not done been one myself. Musicians respect me because I've been there. I do not consider any career maneuver wasted, but as life changes, so do we—and so do our goals.

Though the music business does not put an official ceiling on age, it is as unrealistic to expect to become a top executive at a record label at age 17 as it is to be signed to a major record deal later in life.

The purpose of this book is not to tell you what you can and cannot do with your life and career. However, in determining your goals, you should keep these windows and the "quickly and easily" adage in mind.

SHORT-TERM GOALS

It is imperative that you plot your course with a series of goal lists. A one-year plan, a six-month plan, a one-month plan, and a weekly plan work best for me, but you may prefer different time increments. Put the most important things that you need to do at the top of your list and check them off as they're done.

Weekly

Weekly goal lists should be the map of everything you do connected with your career, such as rehearsing your band, choosing material, going to your voice lessons, reading business-related materials, updating your Web site, networking with other performers or business types, making necessary telephone calls, choosing pictures or costumes, sending press releases and letters of inquiry, and attending auditions. You should include absolutely everything related to your career in these lists. Even though some of the items may seem trivial, they're not because everything you accomplish is a small victory, and it's the small victories that add up to big gains. It will also give you a sense of accomplishment to look over your list and see what you've completed. Finishing your list can help you to feel better about what you're doing and feel better about yourself because you're laying the groundwork for what must be done.

At the end of the week, look at what hasn't been done, and either put it on the next week's list or determine that it's not that important to achieve. Be wary, though, if you have a number of unfinished items; it could mean that you're not working hard enough or that your goal-setting is unrealistic.

The following example is a set of goals or objectives for one week in the management of an unsigned artist's career. This particular week we were preparing for a show; not every week is this intense.

This Week's Goals

- Send letter/tape/press kit to six record labels we've contacted

- Send package/videotape to Reno promoter re: upcoming season's show

- Call Frankie T. at WB Entertainment to follow up show invitation

- Call A&R rep from Island Records to follow up show invitation

- Send press kit to *On the Boulevard* magazine re: concert review

- Finish choreography for new show

- Rehearse dancers on new routines

- Check with merchandising company to make sure T-shirts are ready

- Create and duplicate flyers (1000) for the show

- Have meeting with band drummer and new percussionist

- Finish recording demo of new song

- Complete rough demo tracks for dance rehearsals

Monthly

Monthly goals should be related more to a comprehensive agenda such as ongoing press and public relations campaigns, the creation of mailing lists, advertising efforts, location of venues to perform in, putting together future shows, choosing musicians, and setting up monthly rehearsal schedules. The following example shows monthly goals for one of my artists.

This Month's Goals

- Check band schedules

- Set up rehearsal for October 7 or 8, (one four-hour rehearsal)

- Check out new rehearsal facility

- Get video of the last show from the video tape operator

- Watch/critique video

- Write raps/patter for upcoming show

- Set up appearance for benefit:

    - Call promoter for concert information

    - Call publicity for press releases

- Write press release for festival show

- Call the promoter for a list of other performers

- Design a flyer with press quotes

- Send out 500-piece mailing

- Write/send/follow up press releases for show to:

    - *Music Connection Magazine*

    - *LA Weekly*

    - *New Times*

    - *Buzz Magazine*

- Contact A&R from labels with acts on show

- Follow up calls to:

  - Interscope Records

  - Criterion publishing meeting

  - Arrange lunch meeting with lawyer

  - Dance rehearsal for new routines

Yearly

This is a much bigger picture. If you can tie these goals in with your New Year's resolutions, more power to you. Yearly goals lists could include such items as procuring a record deal, publishing deal or management contract; becoming more visible in your local market; or relocating to another city where the musical opportunities are greater.

The following example is a one-year goal list for a client. Note that there are not as many items on this yearly list as on the weekly or monthly lists because the yearly goals are much more ambitious and far-reaching. This list provided an overview for the entire year's activities and helped us to move the artist's career in the right direction.

This Year's Goals

- Finish 4 songs, master them on 24-track for submission to labels

- Design CD insert for product and duplicate CDs

- Design new press kit to go with CDs

- Set up photo session for shots for press kit

- Perform at five high-profile outdoor summer festivals with a 5,000+ capacity

- Design merchandising campaign for live performance, T-shirts, caps, etc.

- Produce a full production video

- Package and find outlets for video with local television stations in California

- Find legal representation

- Expand network to include more A&R

- Meet more music supervisors to find possible film and TV outlets for songs

- Go out to more music industry events

- Do everything in our power to make this act more signable

If you have a partner, manager, or someone you can trust, these goal-setting techniques will be doubly effective. In order for goal-setting to succeed, there has to be some type of accountability. If you're extremely motivated and disciplined, you may be accustomed to being accountable only to yourself . Most of us aren't that lucky, however, and it helps to have to explain to a second party why something did or didn't get done. You have two options if you're working alone: you can either check off the items yourself on your list, or ask a close friend, spouse, paramour, or confidant to be your conscience. Checking off career-related goals as you accomplish them is very rewarding emotionally and will keep you on the road to success.

ELIMINATE THE NEGATIVE

Fear of Failure

To build skills that will enable you to make contact with others, you must first recognize and control your fear. It's not the fear that a singer gets before going on stage or fears of tangible things—it's a deep rooted insecurity that almost all of us have had since we were children.

In a networking situation, the following factors cause fear:

- Perceived lack of skill

- A need for approval

- A distorted perception of reality

- A poor self-image

- Negative self-talk

When you lack skill, you lack confidence and therefore feel fear. What do you need to learn to be comfortable with others in a music business setting? Is it knowledge about the business? Acquire it. Do you feel inadequate about your lack of success compared with others? Maybe what you're feeling is simple envy. Recognize this for what it is and let it flow through you. It's natural.

The need for approval is one of the most basic requirements of all entertainers. The rest of us, to varying degrees, have this trait as a holdover from childhood. When we meet others, they may or may not accept us based on a variety of perceptions, not all of them under our control. How do you feel when an initial contact isn't friendly? Is it reasonable to expect all of your unknown contacts to be receptive to you? Do you need to change our expectations regarding approval?

It is very easy to prejudge people you have not yet met. You can even talk yourself out of success by imagining all types of negative responses to your efforts to gain a solid footing in the music industry.

Do you often perceive indifference as rejection? It's not; it's a reaction you get from preoccupied or overworked individuals. Don't take it personally, because their reaction has nothing to do with you, but with the circumstances in which you interact.

I wish I had a dollar for every time someone said to me "I called ___Records, (insert Capitol, Def Jam, Warner Bros., etc.), and the receptionist was very rude when I asked if they listened to unsolicited material!" The receptionist wasn't being rude; she was probably dealing with 15 other incoming telephone calls and didn't have time to explain to a novice songwriter how the music industry works. Some songwriters seem to think that everyone in New York, Nashville, or Los Angeles is dying to hear their material. A vague egotistical overstatement of "how much money your company will make" off these unproven works only identifies the speaker as a rank amateur.

Networking is the way to get songs listened to, not blindly calling up and bothering record or publishing companies. Because of the potential liability of nuisance lawsuits, most of the big companies won't listen to unsolicited material anyhow. Get it where it needs to go through creative networking.

Rejection is a Fact of Life in the Music Industry

Songwriters pitch songs to publishers who reject them. Publishers pitch songs to producers who reject them. Producers pitch songs to artists who reject them. Producers and artists pitch finished masters to record companies who reject them, and record companies sell product to consumers who reject them. It's a virtual food chain of rejection, and it's a fact of life. The first time I heard a record company honcho refer to records as "product," I was shocked. The first time a record company A&R man listened to 30 seconds of my song and gave me the bum's rush, I was indignant. Looking back on these experiences, however, I realize they were probably the first moments when I actually began to comprehend the music business.

When creating a popular art form, you have to be constantly aware that you create for a competitive economic marketplace in a specific place and time. If you have pretensions about creating works of art that are beyond such petty economic judgments, you'd better become a poet, playwright, or surrealist painter, not a music industry professional.

Fear of Success

It is much easier to be a failure than to succeed. Fear of success is a self-sabotaging trait that keeps us from achieving our potential. Those who fear success think they shouldn't be doing as well as they're doing right now. They may believe they've been too successful too fast and tell themselves "this can't last." While many people, including some psychologists, think of fear of success as a confidence or self-esteem problem, it's really more deeply rooted than that. The fear of success results from having a preconceived notion of just how difficult things are or how tough it is to succeed. When you don't meet the problems you expected, you achieve more and produce faster.

When this happens, at first you feel happy and have a great sense of accomplishment. But gradually, if you're suffering from the fear of success, you become anxious. Psychologically, you are unprepared to deal with this sudden onset of success.

Like other self-sabotaging fears, fear of success usually stems from your youth and the messages you received from your parents. It can also come from feeling overly respectful of the field in which you work, and feeling that things are more impossible to achieve than they really are.

Everyone has a negative voice inside us, an inner critic. It is essential that you recognize this voice for what it is and learn to silence it when necessary. Your inner critic will tell you things like this:

- Don't bother finishing this song, it's no good.

- No one's going to record this.

- You don't belong here.

- You can't talk to the president of a record company, he'll know you're just a small town hick.

We all have developed ideas about how we should act and how successful we should be. Until we change these ideas and make it okay to succeed, we will continue to sabotage our own efforts. To help change these ideas, it's list time again! Get out your notebook.

List 1: List ten reasons why you deserve a record or publishing deal, a job at a record company, or whatever your end goal may be.

List 2: Write down three things you may be doing to avoid achievement. These could include procrastination, poor planning, having no personal or professional goals, or refusing to apply yourself to your chosen profession.

Discuss these lists with a trusted friend or associate to give you a very truthful "reality check." To succeed, you will have to be able to separate yourself from your ego and take tough criticism. Can you remember events in your life when you felt successful and fulfilled? How did you achieve these results? How were you conditioned to succeed, and what resources did you rely on to achieve your goals?

Use your memory to recall the opposite: moments of inadequacy, fear, or failure. What were your feelings at the time, and why? Many early childhood experiences determine adult emotional reactions. If you can use your memory to recall your experiences, then you can begin to understand why you react as you do. Everyone was once a child, and your inner child can often be held accountable for your deepest feelings and fears. Here are some more tips on helping to get rid of those fears.

- Eliminate the negative people in your life.

- Find and create more reasons to feel good about yourself.

- Visualize your success, imagine yourself being where you want to be, whether it's in the recording studio, onstage, or behind a desk in a record company.

- Remember that your small victories and accomplishments will add up. Make sure that every single day you work, you do something for your career.

- Network with people you respect and observe the way they move, talk, and act.

- Remember that the most successful individuals have doubts, fears, and struggles too.

Negative-Speak

"The record business is run by a bunch of crooks." "A&R people wouldn't know a good song if it bit them on the butt." "My music isn't like that crap on the radio." "I don't write songs for 12-year-old girls to buy at the mall, my music is for people who think."

At one time or another, I've heard all of the above state-ments—and many more—that can be classified as negative-speak. They're clichés that camouflage insecurity on the part of the speaker and negative self-sabotage.

Negative words often have transparent, alternative meanings. If I read the statement, "I hate rap music," I will make certain assumptions about the writer:

- He is racist.

- He is middle-aged.

- He doesn't have the wherewithal to discern a diverse, multilayered genre made up of many components.

- He is not in the music business because the words *music* and *hate* are not compatible in the same sentence.

If a particular type of music does not speak to you that's a different story—not all of us can understand every genre, be it rap, country, or polka. But personally, I'd be very hesitant to work with someone who professed to me that they "hated" any form of music.

We really do have the power to change the negative to positive, but first we must become aware of this power. Most intelligent readers will agree that positive thoughts bring positive results and negative thoughts bring negative results, but they have trouble making this concept work in their own lives and careers.

It's always easier to say something bad than to say something good. Even writing this book, I've had to identify my own negative thoughts and energies and concentrate on the positive. It would certainly be much easier for me to relate horror stories to you about the inner workings of the music industry, bad deals I've seen go down, and the strangeness of the participants, but we can't concern ourselves with this; it's too negative.

You can't avoid negative thoughts and feelings; they're all too human. What you can do is try to find the lessons that can be learned from all situations, to believe that ultimately you can succeed, to minimize setbacks while concentrating on the big picture, and to learn from your mistakes.

In the entertainment world, there is a certain type of personality that succeeds. Len Chandler, co-founding director of the Los Angeles Songwriters Showcase, former Columbia recording artist, and 40-year veteran of the music wars, emphasizes that one of the keys to success is "to be the type of person that other people want to help to succeed." This statement is blindingly clear. It's true: The further up the ladder you go, the nicer people tend to be.

Music Biz Myth #5: *In order to appear important, you have to throw your weight around and immediately establish your verbal superiority.*

The Facts: It's often the smallest fish that tend to be the most obnoxious cretins and have the largest egos. In many cases, their prime motivation is insecurity. To appear in your best light, be polite and gracious and be considerate of other's feelings and abilities. Don't let yourself be tread on, but don't spread attitude around. Don't create a negative vibe around yourself. One of the first ways you're judged is by your personality and energy. Enthusiasm and being positive are qualities that attract others to you. Cultivate these traits to maximize your success.

Show business is made up of people who have successfully reinvented themselves. When Bob Dylan appeared on the folk scene in the early 1960s, he'd invented a new persona, name, and history for himself, emulating his hero, Woody Guthrie. Madonna is a prime example of an entertainer who has successfully ascertained her audience's expectations and then exceeded them. Bruce Springsteen developed an audience by capitalizing on his "everyman" image, then transformed himself from an emaciated Jersey shore bar rat to a strapping, guitar-wielding rock'n'roll love god. Michael Jackson reinvented his face, and Janet Jackson transforms her image with each video in which she appears.

In show business, your visual appearance is vital to your presentation. It's not enough to simply be good looking. In fact, many of the heroes of rock'n'roll music don't have this particular advantage, but a sense of style is a necessity. The best style is quite obviously the one that you alone have, but look for guidelines. Check out fashion industry magazines for style tips, but be sure that the way you present yourself is not inappropriate and ludicrous. Also, don't appear to be too obviously trendy—we all blanch when we see old pictures of ourselves, but sometimes it's just the styles of clothing we're reacting to.

About Your Self-Image

Do you see yourself as a professional in the music business? Self-image is a barometer that you can manipulate any way you wish. The way that you perceive yourself is exactly the way you will be perceived by others, because positioning must first happen in your mind before it can happen in the minds of those with whom you meet and network.

Your physical appearance is strongly related to your self-image. A visual package based on the foundations of physical exercise, proper diet, and good grooming techniques all say to the people that you meet that you care about yourself and what you do. In business, severely overweight people might be judged as out of control and very thin people judged as having eating disorders.

Excellent physical condition projects a good first impression for several reasons. First, it indicates high self-esteem because a person who abuses his body is likely to have a poor opinion of himself. Second, it indicates discipline because, for most of us, it is no easy task to maintain a good physique. Third, it provides stamina and extra energy.

In the past decade, the image of the musician/producer as a drugged and alcohol-besotted individual has given way to one who is lean, trim, and tough. Executives in their late 50s project an attitude of youthful vigor, and rock stars can play four-hour shows without the aid of stimulants.

These factors are controllable only by you, but you have to want to be in control. If you give up any element of control, you're telegraphing signals that you don't like yourself.

And if you don't like yourself, don't expect others to.

How to Change What You Don't Like

First, define what is changeable and what is not.

Hair color, eye color (via contact lenses), and muscle definition are all subject to change. If it's a physical transformation you desire, ask yourself why you feel you need to change. While managing talent, I've observed that many times the best-looking individuals are the least secure about their looks. Instead of drastically changing your appearance, concentrate on the cultivation of a style that is uniquely your own.

There are professionals to help you do whatever you wish: hair stylists, weight trainers, clothing color specialists, etc. There are churches, hypnotherapists, psychologists, mediums, and spiritualists to aid you in your spiritual development. There are libraries, books, schools, and classes to educate you.

The healthiest and most effective way to change anything about yourself is by changing your attitude. Learn to change all that you can in the interest of your career, but also accept the things about yourself that you can't change.

Your verbal skills are being evaluated constantly when you interact with others. Do you hate the sound of your speaking voice on tape? Then practice sounding the way you think you should sound. Demosthenes, the famous Greek orator of ancient times, practiced speaking above the roar of the ocean with a mouthful of pebbles to strengthen his vocal skills. Pretty extreme stuff, but the point is, any sound that can be made can be changed. On the telephone, your verbal skills will determine whether or not you get through to the right people, so you need to sound confident, educated, articulate, relaxed, and very polite. Working with a tape recorder and a qualified voice teacher can make your voice more effective. If you know you sound good, you'll be more likely to have self-esteem and confidence.

I once received a call at my office from a young lady who was in town from Canada and had been referred to me by a PR friend. She began our conversation by asking, "Is it true that the music business is all about who you know?" When I answered in the affirmative, her whiny tone became more pronounced. "I've been calling record companies and publishers, and they say they don't accept unsolicited materials. I don't want to pay a music lawyer $900 an hour [note: I don't know a single lawyer who charges that much!] to pitch my songs. What can I do?" At this point in the conversation I told her the truth: I had turned her off at the beginning of our conversation because of the negative tone in her voice and the fact that she was soliciting "no" answers. I suspect that everyone she spoke with on the telephone had exactly the same response.

You will receive reflected positive responses from people whom you approach in an upbeat, positive manner. Your honest enthusiasm about a song, an opportunity, an act, or an artist is something that can't be faked. Bluster and overhype are immediate turnoffs, but the energy generated by your reaction to what you truly believe can be felt by others and can actually open doors for you that would otherwise be locked.

Show business is made up of self-centered people. An honest absorption in your project is to be expected, but never allow this to blind you to what other people are doing. When you encounter contacts in business or socially, it's absolutely imperative to find out what they're doing because:

- Your interest in their project will be balanced by their interest in yours.

- It makes them feel good that you care.

- It gives them a chance to toot their own horn.

- If they're doing something positive, there may be an opportunity for you to become involved.

An invaluable law of human conduct is to always make the other person feel important. To quote William James, "The deepest principle in human nature is the craving to be appreciated."

Remember the old adage "birds of a feather flock together"? Like many hoary old clichés, this one is painfully true. Friendship is vital to a productive life. Indeed, it's friendships that form your most vital network, so don't set yourself up for failure by hanging around with losers.

Losers are individuals whose negativity affects you adversely. They're quite often people who can think of a thousand ways that something won't work and have predetermined attitudes about people they don't know and places where they haven't been. They know the music business is a corrupt game run by gangsters. They can always tell you what you did wrong in performance, why your song is not up to par, or why the world is too ignorant to recognize their particular brand of genius. In business, they're the people who are wasted in their present positions, aren't paid enough to be slogging through the mire that they're in, and would be much further up the ladder if there was any justice in this rotten world.

These people are excess baggage and a waste of your time. Cut them loose, now.

To be the type of person other people want to see succeed, you've first got to first project the image of a winner. Have a sense of humor and show your contacts that you have a human side and can discuss a variety of topics, not just yourself and your latest achievements. Show an honest interest in people and your shared reality in the world around you. Don't sell constantly, don't brag, don't run down other people, smile, give off a high energy charm. Work on developing your conversational skills.

Since your network will be made up of people you consider friends, develop your friendship skills by sending cards and thank you notes and letting others know that you appreciate them and what they do for you.

What They See: Personal Appearance

Clothing in a music business office usually consists of one or more of the following:

- Promotional T-shirts on both men and women

- Assorted piercings, including earrings, nose rings, and pierced eyebrows on both men and women

- Current hair styles (shaved, buzzed, dreadlocks, multicolored etc.)

- Four-day beard growth

- Tattoos

- Sports coats thrown artlessly over the aforementioned T-shirts

- Hats

- Leather jackets and boots

- Van Dykes and goatees

Now imagine a young executive "dressed for success" walking into this environment. He'd immediately be judged as a "suit," an outsider. Coats and ties are OK, but use individuality in making your selections. A dress suit is only appropriate when dealing with lawyers or finance officers of record companies. This is good news for those of us without a lot of money, because style, fortunately, is free. You can use a variety of outlets, including the old standby, the used clothing store, to have fun and create an identity for yourself. Visuals do more than just make an immediate impression—they also help make you memorable. It's not just your physical appearance, but the clothing that adorns it that makes people remember you.

Try these wearing any of the following:

- Lapel pins (they're good for starting conversations)

- Big men's sports coats on women

- A hat

- Bow-ties

- Ties in general

- A complete outfit from another decade

- Vintage shoes

- For women: something not normally used or thought of as a purse to carry your paraphernalia in

- For men: a vintage used briefcase

- Ethnic scarves

A coherent, recognizable style that's related to the music you create or represent is best. Cohesion is the obvious goal. One of the artists I manage can create a subtle impact simply by walking into a crowded restaurant in Hollywood. It's not because of overstatement, it's that his look is singular, natural, and unique, and he looks the part of a pop star. If you're a hip-hop, rock, or reggae artist, you must look like one—but be sure to add to the "uniform" with your own personal touches, or you're simply imitating what others have done.

I once attended a music business seminar where a young woman was complaining that she wasn't taken seriously in the music business and men were always hitting on her in business situations. At the end of the class when she stood up to leave the room, I observed that she was wearing a shorter-than-short leather skirt, high heels, and a see-through blouse. Her blond hair came from a bottle and her gait, no doubt affected by her spike-heeled shoes, was reminiscent of a lady of the night sashshaying down Sunset Boulevard.

Women in the music business—a male-dominated arena where some of the men are prone to adolescent sexual behavior—have to be very careful what signals they give off when trying to be taken seriously as an artist or a business person. This is not to say that you need to dress puritanically, but since the area of male/female relations is tricky, don't add to the obstacles by sending out easily misinterpreted messages.

I had a phone call from a female singer/dancer who had been referred to me by her voice teacher. She knew we were auditioning backup singers for one of my clients and was eager to be involved. I told her that we had decided to use only male singers, but she sounded like an interesting person, so I asked her to send me a tape, résumé, and bio both because I was interested in what she did professionally and to keep on file for upcoming opportunities. Her response floored me: "You producers are all alike," she said, "you just want to go out with me." Keep in mind that she'd never met me and we were on the phone so I couldn't see her; she may well have resembled my Uncle Henry for all I knew.

I would never consider subjecting my acts, musicians, or crew to someone who had such an attitude, because music is a co-operative effort and requires the correct chemistry between many people. In a band or show situation, an incorrect attitude from one person can severely throw off the entire balance of the rest of the group.

Probably this singer/dancer had a bad experience, and I can certainly sympathize with her—however, not all men in the music industry are pigs.

Men and women who rely on an overtly sexual physical presentation don't usually have much going for them in any other areas, or they are so insecure that they're forced to rely on attributes other than musical ones.

What To Wear Where!

When I first accepted the position as advertising director for a songwriter publication, I went out on sales calls dressed in a promotional rock'n'roll T-shirt with faded jeans, a leather jacket, a three-day growth of beard, and an earring, and I got the sales. I was selling advertising space to small-scale recording studio owners, and, in my experience, this was how they dressed during daytime hours. By dressing like them, I gained their trust. I read all the technology magazines for studio owners, I knew all of the latest equipment, and I could recognize the outboard and recording gear on sight.

It's a pretty well-known sales trick that you have to look the part, and the more you can resemble the person you're selling to, the better your chances of closing the sale. This technique can backfire though, so you'll have to research your prospects. A good rule of thumb: when in doubt whether to dress up or down, dress up. It's better to appear a little classier than to be viewed as a bum.

For entertainers, the trick is to always dress like you're something special, because you are.

P.S.: Don't wear sunglasses indoors unless you're Yoko Ono, Bono, or Ray Charles.

What to Wear to a Meeting with a Club Owner

Club owners are indeed curious beasts. I have been fortunate to work for some of the best and to have avoided most of the worst. Keep in mind that the club owner has only one priority: to sell drinks. If you can do this, fine, if not your career will be short-lived.

Mixed signals can work well for the musician/business person. Try crossing over conventional stage gear with a sports coat. Since you're playing two roles, you have to present both in your attire. For nice clubs dress up, but define your show biz position by being just a little flashier, and let your appearance indicate that you can take charge, command attention, and conduct yourself like a professional.

What to Wear to a Meeting with a Lawyer or Manager

Let their personal style dictate yours. Most music business lawyers do not dress casually, especially if they have offices with more conservative older partners. While it's true that some of the younger lawyers in Los Angeles dress much like rock'n'roll musicians, they're far outnumbered by the more conservative dressers. A lawyer is a vital part of your team in any music industry contractual dealings, and they generally work on the retainer system. You should look like someone who'll pay your bill on time and who knows how to take care of business. A coat and tie for men is not inappropriate.

With managers, it's a mixed bag. I've seen high-level managers in shorts and Hawaiian shirts, and I've seen them in Pierre Cardin suits. At a recent black-tie award dinner, I observed the manager of a 16 million record–selling act dressed as if he was working in his yard. But managers are very much their own people, and theoretically, they don't have to answer to anyone except their artists. If you're an entertainer, look like an entertainer; but in Los Angeles it's generally assumed that it's the "wanna be's" who overdress, not the heavy hitters.

Record company A&R people are usually out in the clubs till all hours. They're overworked, underpaid rock'n'roll survivors, and they look it. The hipness quotient in this field is very high, and most of the descriptions earlier in this chapter of record company apparel apply to A&R and publicity personnel. If you're invited to meet label employees as an artist, show respect in your apparel, but don't overdress. A sports coat without a tie works fine.

What to Wear to a Music Industry Conventions

As a producer of the Songwriters Expo, the world's largest educational and discovery event held for songwriters, I could always spot the amateurs and the out-of-towners. They were the ones who looked uncomfortable in their clothes, were overdressed for ten hours of walking and sitting in classes and workshops, and attempted to look overly hip with flashy clothes and footwear impractical for traversing the halls and expansive distances of the convention center where the event was held.

At conventions, a conversation piece is essential. You'll be meeting a lot of strangers, and having something for them to focus on gives them something to begin speaking to you about. Many people are shy and insecure in these settings and need a reason to speak with you. They may be dying to do so, and the strange little tchotchke you have in your lapel may be the key.

CHAPTER 5

Selling Your Stuff

ales are a fact of business life. It can be as simple as the process of buying a soda at the corner market or as complex as creating multinational corporations to market records. In the pop music world, rock'n'roll, R&B, Latin, and country concerts are sponsored by companies who have determined, through market research, that the audiences for these types of music are also the primary buyers of their products. We see pop stars pitching soda pop and lending their names to lines of shoes and clothing.

The skills that you develop in sales, and your comprehension of how necessary these skills are, can help you achieve success. In the music business, you will be selling yourself and the music you represent to:

• Other performers/musicians

• Record companies

• Audiences

• Publishers

• Club owners

• Promoters

• Managers

• Agents

In this chapter, you will learn how to call attention to and how to sell yourself. We will explore ways to give your project wings via the creation of a "scene" and how to convince the media to cover it. We'll look at examples of press releases and bios that have proven to be interesting enough to be included in major magazines and newspapers. Using your current skills and abilities, you can also discover how to barter creatively to save yourself thousands of dollars while widening your network and advancing your career.

SELLING YOURSELF FROM YOUR HOMETOWN

It used to be that bands and musicians had to move to New York, Nashville, or Los Angeles to become successful. Not anymore. Even though these three cities continue to be the recording and media capitols of the U.S., there is a strong regional backbone to success in the music business. Over the last couple of decades, pop music scenes have become prominent in such unlikely places as Athens, Georgia; Akron, Ohio; Minneapolis, and Seattle.

Record companies like to see are strong economics on a local or regional level. Your chances of signing a one million dollar contract with Warner Brothers are much greater if you can sell 10,000 copies of your CD regionally while performing in your local area. Believe me, if you can accomplish this feat, there will be someone dying to speak with you.

There are many levels of success in the music business. You can be successful locally, regionally, nationally, or internationally. Let's assume, though, that national and international recognition is the ultimate prize. Here's one possible scenario: Your band meets in your hometown and begins playing local schools, teen clubs, and events. Using a local recording studio (maybe on a partial "speculation deal" in which the studio owner gives you free studio time in exchange for a piece of your publishing action or a percentage of your signing advance when you sign a contract with a major record label), you record CDs for distribution at your gigs, use the money from the sales to create T-shirts, and use the funds accrued from both of these activities to make a video. In the meantime, the local radio station becomes involved and begins to sponsor regional appearances for your band and plays your songs on the air. With the video, you can use local television outlets to generate sponsorship interest from local businesses in your region.

Your band continues to broaden its performance base, venturing further and further from your hometown. You use your extensive audience to generate a database to promote upcoming shows and new products. All of your CDs and merchandise come with "bounceback" materials, so your buyers can order more and varied forms of merchandise. Your band also creates a Web site and a newsletter to announce upcoming shows and advertise new products. You involve sponsors on local, regional, and national levels who have a desire to be visible to the particular demographic group (which you can identify through market research—questions you ask in your newsletter and on your Web site about their buying habits). You also create links to your sponsors from your Web site.

Management would be very attracted by the initiative shown by your band; so would a record label. Since your group has already proven itself, you will be much less of a risk to a record company who could conceivably invest hundreds of thousands of dollars in your success. You will have also have proven that there is a market for what you're doing and that you are aggressive and resourceful enough to go for it.

Don't rule out local opportunities; it is often possible to make contact with major music business players through conferences and by meeting them when they are on tour with shows. Hang out in the hotel lobby, talk your way backstage. Also, major record labels are in touch with the retail outlets in virtually every city in the country.

Local contacts are essential. Make sure to include the following in your list of people to meet, cultivate friendships with, and make aware of what you're doing:

- **Local print and electronic media.** Local radio stations often have shows and produce events featuring local talent, which you could use to give your act credibility and visibility. Local newspapers, magazines, and freebies can also make you more visible and give you the all important "clips" for your press kit. Keep in mind that in order to entice the media, you need a strong, focused visual package, great pictures (particularly action shots), bios, logos, and a cover letter. These will make them more interested in giving you space in their publications.

It is also much easier to get press if you're doing something newsworthy. Performing for local charities is a wonderful source of exposure for budding acts; local video shows are bursting out all over and need local celebrities with video product.

- **Concerts and clubs.** Performing as an opening act for touring groups is a proven method of furthering your career. The headlining band's management, agents, and contacts can be valuable. Performing in clubs can be a good starting point for a career, but if your ultimate goal is to be a concert act, you can never start early enough. Fairs, street festivals, and carnivals often have a big-time concert atmosphere, plus they have a large built in audience. If you can convince organizers to let you play, even for free, you can cover your expenses by selling CDs and T-shirts. You can also use these particular opportunities to create your mailing list, by having sign-up sheets ready to be filled out by audience members.

- **Recording studios.** What a great place to meet music people. There's an art to hanging out in the studios, though. The main thing is to keep out of the way, keep your mouth shut, don't put anything on the console (ever!!!), and be supportive. Also, don't give your advice unless you're asked. The best way to be in the studio is if you're wanted, needed, or working there—interning has a long and time-honored tradition of opening doors. Do everything in your power to be around the studio environment; it's the best place to learn about music as a recorded medium.

- **Video facilities.** These are a close second to recording studios for meeting musicians, managers, players, and bands. Again, if you can work there, even for free, take the opportunity. There's a whole set of equipment and a language you'll need to master. See it first hand. There is always a place for someone to help at the shoot.

- **Personal relationships.** These are the key to successful networking. Cultivate every opportunity to meet people. Be sincere, be honest, be the kind of person others want to meet. Other musicians and songwriters can provide not only obvious economic opportunities, but also a much-needed emotional support system.

START YOUR OWN ORGANIZATION

If you want to be part of a music industry group and don't have one in your area, maybe you should take the initiative and start one. What you need is a common focus, ways of finding and contacting potential members, a place to hold your initial get-togethers, a theme, and a name, and you're off.

I was invited, along with assorted record company personnel and music publishers, to the desert community of Palm Springs to speak to an organization that was just forming. Palm Springs is not a previously known hotbed of musical action (unless you count the late Liberace), but the community is close enough to Los Angeles to allow residents the opportunity to visit there often. A diverse group of writers came out to present strong, consistent material. The hook to this event was that by bringing in publishers to evaluate the songs and pick them up for possible signings, there was an immediate focus and possible reward. The sponsoring organization brought in a local radio station to act as a sponsor and persuaded their community newspaper to donate ad space and a leading local hotel to put us all up for free. The event was very rewarding for all of the participants, but best of all, the Palm Spring locals succeeded in founding an organization and are now able to network among themselves.

Starting a networking organization gives you an obvious reason to contact executives in the music business, and you can ultimately work your own agenda into that of the organization. You can use the greater power of the group to promote events focusing on your music or bands with which you're involved. You can use your invitations and make overtures to key players in the music industry to form the relationships so vital to success in the business. You can make your name known and your influence felt much more effectively with the power of an organization behind you.

CREATE A SCENE

Virtually every important trend in pop music has come out of a "scene." Liverpool and San Francisco in the 1960s, New York in the 1970s, Minneapolis and Athens, Georgia in the 1980s, and Seattle and in the 1990s—in all these locations, music tied together with fashion, locale, and a specific sense of time and place to create a scene. Having a scene or being a part of one has many advantages. The first is that it provides a network of people to work with. The press is attracted to a scene because it gives them a handle, something they can name, and an opportunity to write about the influences, personalities, sociology, and fashion of what's around the music. Audiences are also attracted to a scene because it gives them an opportunity to become a part of what they deem is "happening." Record companies are attracted to bands that come out of scenes because they recognize there is already interest in what's being created; hence, there's a buying populace and momentum which, if marketed correctly, could trigger a national phenomenon.

Eight Necessary Ingredients to the Creation of a Scene

1. An open-minded progressive audience (preferably college-age or younger)

2. Enough bands to sustain interest

3. Supportive press, preferably nonmainstream

4. Venues at which to present artists

5. A specific sense of style and fashion singular to the music

6. Graphic artists, video personnel, and photographers to capture the picture

7. Visionaries and high energy leaders

8. A sense of community among creative people

If you can't identify or be a part of a preexistent scene, I strongly suggest that you band together with others to create your own. The way to do this begins with your thinking of the big picture, not just your next week's gig. Target your act to a group of buyers, send regular press releases and newsletters to mailing lists, display flyers and posters at locales where your strongest audience is found. T-shirts, caps, buttons, and bumper stickers turn the wearers into walking billboards for your act. Ads in local papers, music magazines, or on radio and television stations can often be gotten for free if you bring the media in as a cosponsor of your events. When creating a scene, you have to be event-oriented rather than just going from week to week and performing for a limited audience.

It is helpful to have physical hangouts for scene members to gather and exchange ideas. When I interviewed record producer Roger Bechirian (who has produced Squeeze, Elvis Costello, and Nick Lowe), he shared his memories of London in the mid-'70s, when the Sex Pistols were shaking up the world of rock'n'roll. The physical center of that scene happened to be the Pistol's manager's leatherwear shop, Sex, in London. Many times these centralizing locales are the clubs where the bands play, record stores, or even the offices of the magazines that write about them.

I was in New York City in 1975 when the punk movement exploded out of CBGB's, a tiny, smelly bar on the Bowery. Groups like Television, Talking Heads, Blondie, and the Ramones played there every night. There was a strong sense of community among the bands and a common language of alienation and urban chaos. The scene gained national recognition in a very short time.

Form a community with your local musicians: share information, music, experiences, rehearsal halls, and gigs. When Jane's Addiction leader Perry Farrell visualized the first Lollapalooza Tour, he brought rock, metal, alternative, and rap artists together in a phenomenal show which was the biggest event going. Even though the audiences for these bands were diverse, the bands were all working outside of the commercial mainstream, had strong messages, and a political orientation. By involving local organizations and giving political and environmental groups booths, the tour achieved a grand scale and affected audiences emotionally, musically, and politically—and it made a big heap o' money, to boot.

Lilith Fair succeeded in promoting the careers of female artists—including Sarah MacLachlan, Alanis Morissette and Jewel—while making a dynamic political and cultural statement. Other large scale tours have exposed different artists' audiences to each other with similar dramatic success.

Although you may not have national bands as your contacts, this approach will work locally. Look for common threads with other bands, musicians, writers, and audiences. Exploit these connections, make the total bigger than the individual elements, and everyone wins.

COMING IN SIDEWAYS

One of the realities of being in a music capitol is that it's hard to earn money performing. If you're used to working in clubs to earn a living wage in your home area, you'll be shocked when your band is asked to pay $900 to perform in some sleazy club in New York or L.A. It's simply a matter of supply and demand; if supply is up, demand is down. In a city where there are literally thousands of musicians fighting for visibility, there are few opportunities to make a living wage in clubs. The $100 per night per player or so you might make in Cleveland, Ohio, as a working musician is nonexistent in the big city. Consequently, if you're moving to a major music center, unless you're financially independent, you may need to get a day job.

The best type of day job for music people is one doesn't require a lot of your time or creativity, is flexible, and has a negligible commitment on your part. Waiter and waitress gigs are perfect for this (in L.A., we talk about the quintessential "actor/singer/model/dancer/waiter"). When I first came to Los Angeles, I worked in a phone sales position. Not high on the prestige ladder to be sure, but I made enough to survive, worked only mornings, and no one was even aware I was working a straight job, since I didn't schedule any music sessions until I got off work at noon. People just assumed that I was a night owl. Best of all though, most of the other people working there were also music business people, and we could network and exchange information to help each other out.

Working at the same unholy sales job (which was actually selling after-dinner mints to Ma'n'Pa stores and restaurants—eek!) was a woman singer whom I recognized from her nightly appearances on a syndicated television game show. When I inquired why she was working such a lowly job, she explained that it took two weeks out of the year to shoot all of the season's episodes, so she still had 50 weeks left to work. So much for the glamour of television!

For aspiring recording artists in particular, it's probably better not to announce to everyone how you make a living. Be subtly enigmatic, because what people imagine you do for money is probably much more interesting than the truth.

If you're a future mogul working at a straight job, be sure that you're able to access your incoming phone calls and messages to give the appearance that you're running a full-time management or production company, even if you're slaving away for someone else. An answering service or pager/voice mail are alternatives that can allow you to miss phone calls and still be professional.

Other hopefuls aspire to jobs in the business itself. The mail room is the starting place for many people (including David Geffen, who began his legendary career there at the William Morris agency) and is still a way in, although nowadays, jobs in the mail room at the Morris Agency require a college degree. And many record and music companies have adopted a new policy and won't hire songwriters or performers to work in their offices or will refuse to listen to submissions from their employees.

On the local or regional level, record store jobs can offer valuable music business experience. You can meet promo people from the various labels, come into contact with marketing companies, and see firsthand what type of promotion and product will make buyers walk away with the latest CD clutched in their eager hands.

Radio stations are also good break-in points to observe how this end of the business works, to find out what records get played, and why. Working for a local concert promoter may offer valuable contacts for future endeavors, as well as educating you about the realities of the touring business.

The touring business itself is the modern equivalent of running away with the circus. It's hectic, it's crazy, the money is bad, the coffee is worse, and the hours are intolerable. But for someone aspiring to the management or production end of the business, it's quite an education to go out on a concert tour as a roadie or a technical person.

The Business of the Business

There's the record business, which is the recording, sale, and manufacturing of music, and there's the music business, which includes everything else. Here in Los Angeles, we see hundreds of cottage industries that are satellites to the music business. Recording and demo studios help performers and writers put their materials into listenable, salable form. Producers, arrangers, and musicians are available to help with the process. Photographers and video technicians document the music visually. Clothing experts, hair stylists, photographers, and image consultants work with labels and artists in creating a strong visual presentation. Public relations consultants and bio writers work with bands, press agents, and publicists to help them promote their gigs. Web designers create appealing online promotions. Artists and musicians can study with vocal instructors and live performance consultants in classroom and studio situations. Journalists document the scene, and thousands of people make their living off the needs of the aspirant.

In your local market, consider niche marketing, that is, establish yourself by doing what no one else is doing. I've seen it work for many people in the music capitals who had the foresight and imagination to create their own role. People become important because they act important. Niche marketing and cottage industries are a way to meet artists and to get in on the ground floor of their developing careers.

Music Publications

If you can write, you may be someone who the music business not only accepts, but actually needs. Jon Landau, Bruce Springsteen's manager, began his career with the Boss as a journalist for *Rolling Stone*. Writing about acts for your local rock rag immediately puts you in the flow of things and gets you in touch with breaking trends in the music business, as well as with the publicity departments of the record labels, artist management, and the acts themselves. It can also give you local notoriety and access to all sorts of entertainment, information, record release parties, and people. You'll actually be invited to these affairs and have opportunities to move into other sectors via the written word.

Start by contacting your local music and entertainment publications to determine their policies on working with freelancers. Be observant of the editorial styles of the publication to which you're submitting work and think about what you may be able to add journalistically to reinforce the magazine's viewpoint. Also, take note of what may be missing from a magazine that you can write about. For example, I became the world music contributor to an L.A.-based music magazine simply by observing that no one was writing about these vibrant global forms. It was as easy as calling and submitting an article.

Once you begin freelancing for one magazine you'll have "clips," or copies of articles you've created, to audition your abilities for others. The more publications you can write for, the more extensive your influence. If you believe in your ability to write, don't be afraid to do it on spec (meaning they buy the piece after you've written it if they like it).

Many music writers often begin to play the other side of the fence—since they understand how the press works they can begin to do public relations and provide publicity services for acts they may meet. Although it is frowned upon (as well as unethical) to write articles about acts you represent, odds are you'll be able to network with other writers who will offer the journalistic support that you, because of potential conflict of interest, are unable to provide. They may have the same needs also.

Magazines are ultimately ruled by advertising dollars. Articles that can reinforce the positions of their strongest advertisers are always welcome. Any article that makes the magazine more appealing to a wider group of buyers will certainly be of interest, because this information can help to convince advertisers to gamble precious advertising dollars to reach consumers.

Another quick way into the publication world is by selling advertising space. This is generally a commission job, but if you need valuable hours to work on music projects, are self-motivated, disciplined, and aggressive, this is a way to make money while being part of the big picture.

Music Biz Myth #6: *If I can work full time, I can make more money, which I can then invest in my career.*

The Facts: Don't make too much money at your straight gig. When I first went to New York, I naively asked someone, "What happens to all of the people who come here to be successful and aren't?" He informed me that many of them took straight jobs to pay the rent and became discouraged at their lack of progress in show business. Meanwhile, they kept moving up the ladder at their straight jobs and began to like the lifestyle that more money could give them. They eventually blended into the populace at large.

If you do what you do in the hope of accruing vast sums of money, please don't go into the music business—there are easier ways to afford a BMW.

We all have limited energies and creativity; if you expend them on behalf of someone else's business, you're short-changing yourself. Sure, it's possible to work at any number of things and make enough money to have a comfortable lifestyle, but if you want success in the music business (which will ultimately pay off in emotional satisfaction as well as monetary gain), you can't give up your vision and creativity. Guard them jealously, and use them to fuel your ambitions.

BARTERING

I was fortunate to get to executive-produce a video that was edited at a major motion picture studio in L.A. on a sound-stage using equipment that cost more than the annual budgets of many emerging nations. Know how much we paid for the facility? Nothing. It was free. How can this be?

Recording studios and engineers need product to demonstrate what they do. An artist on the move can demonstrate equipment and facilities to great advantage for technicians. Songwriters need demos of their songs, singers need tapes of their voices in the studio. This is a proven method of marrying two needs so that everybody wins. The reason we were at the studio was that someone who worked on a network TV show had started their own film company and needed video product to show off his abilities. I happened to manage an artist who needed a dynamite video, so it was a match that worked.

Photographers can always use a visually interesting person for their portfolio, so it's often possible to get 8x10s for just the price of the film and developing. In order to effectively barter, the persons involved must not only need each other, but must be equally qualified.

Many successful musicians are great barterers. I've seen the "You play on my demo and I'll play on yours" trick worked to great advantage. And no band wants to be seen schlepping their equipment onstage, so some rock bands roadie for their friend's bands at special gigs in exchange for their friend's band doing the same for them.

I have a client who is a vocalist and vocal instructor. Whenever he performs at showcase clubs in Los Angeles his band features many of the "first call" players in town. He doesn't have to pay them for their participation in his show, but he does give them vocal lessons. Of course, he has to use players who need vocal lessons (you can't barter with something that the other party doesn't need), but within his network he's been very successful at using players who can use his services too.

When I lived in New York, I hooked up with an audio engineering school who needed guinea pigs so their students could learn how to record and mix music in the studio. Since my band always needed development time and great demos, we were able to work with the students who were learning their chops at the same time that we were learning about arranging and recording in major facilities. In this way, we got 24-track demos of our stuff to shop around.

Many recording studios will hire "second" engineers to work for very little money. To keep these people working, they will give them free access to "down" time, or time which isn't booked, to work on their own projects. Since most recording engineers aspire to produce, if you can hook up with someone in this position, you can both benefit by letting them practice their producing on your band in exchange for your access to that free access to the studio.

Because many of your contacts are also searching for outlets for their own creativity, you need only meet enough ambitious people to form your network of contacts. It's your job to create the energy and momentum around your projects, to be able to sell the vision to potential collaborators and investors, and to create a vehicle which others want to climb onto because it looks like it's going somewhere.

We all have individual paths to walk to achieve success; if we can walk that road with others, it makes the way much less lonely.

Talents/Services to Barter within Your Network

• Computer skills

• Telephone/telemarketing

• Public relations

- Carpentry (I know a musician who helped build a recording studio in exchange for studio time for his own projects. He was also allowed to sell time to his contacts at a discount.)

- Music or voice teaching

- Electric/wiring

- MIDI/programming

- Child care

- Massage therapy

- Proficiency in another language

- Dance or choreography teaching

- Graphic design/art

- Photography/darkroom

- Makeup/hair design

- Owning a truck

- Writing

- Gardening

- Catering/cooking

- Pet care

- Instrument repair

- Furniture refinishing

I compiled this list from talking with real people about their experiences. Each of these services were bartered for recording and video editing time, voice lessons, or the services of technicians and musicians. But bartering requires creativity, not only in evaluating what you have to barter, but also in knowing how to approach contacts within your network—in a word, salesmanship—a topic we'll cover later in this chapter.

Of course, you can't barter for everything. At some point, you will need to put money into your career to realize a return. Whether that money is your own or someone else's depends on several factors, including the extent of your own personal resources and how successful you are in getting investors excited about your career. No one will invest in your career if you haven't bothered to do so yourself. Networking is the best way to assure that your money is being well spent, that you're using creative bartering to offset many of your expenses, and that your project has gained enough momentum so that others wish to ride the magic bandwagon. The truth is, it's necessary to put out, to cast your bread upon the waters, to impress, and particularly, to launch an act.

Just as no magic person will fly from the woodwork to help you make a career, neither will a magic person give you money without some serious terms behind it. Outside investors can be very expensive. In a business as speculative as the music business, there is obviously a greater chance for failure than there is for having money returned, or a profit made. I've seen family and friends become involved in artist's careers, and I've seen hard feelings, emotional upset, and distrust evolve from mishandled and badly accounted for funds.

If you are planning to ask any of your networking contacts for funds, be as professional as possible in putting together a business-like proposal. You'll have a much better chance of raising money for you project if:

• You have a track record of success

• You have a clear-cut business plan

• The funds are for a specific endeavor, such as a video, a 24-track master, to subsidize a concert tour, not just general funds

• You can establish a payback plan

It is in your own best interests to have a cap on the repayment of any investment funds from outside investors. For example, if an investor gives you $10,000 and you agree to pay him 20 percent of your earnings over a year's time, you could end up repaying much more than his initial investment plus interest. Limit his percentage of your future earnings.

The more of your earnings you can retain control of, the healthier and wealthier you'll be in the long run. I've seen acts go into their first record deal owing so much money (not to mention the recoupables that the record company advances them) that they would have to sell back-to-back platinum records to see a single penny in profit.

Initially, the best money to invest in your project is your own. If you want to make millions in the music business, how much money are you willing to invest to make that happen? And if you won't invest in your own career, don't expect others to.

Do Not Spend Your Money on the Following:

- Songsharks, those people who ask you to pay to have your songs recorded for release. These folks work the copyright lists in Washington, D.C., to find names, then invite you to send in your songs for review. You will then receive a congratulations letter announcing your inclusion on their upcoming album. They will ask you for money. Don't send it, tear up their letters immediately. These companies have nothing to do with the legitimate music business.

- Lists of agents and managers

- Home addresses of stars

- Having your song played on the radio

- Having your band included on a compilation album unless you know the company, their history, and their outlets for the record. There are good compilations, and there are bad ones.

- Appearing on a television program (particularly public access)

- Performing in a club (though bands may be asked to sell tickets).

- A music business consultant who claims to be able to use his contacts to get your tape in the proverbial "right hands." There is an unscrupulous operator in Los Angeles who typically bilks unsuspecting bands out of $8,000 at a time. What he does is not technically illegal, so he continues to prosper. Often his victims are so ashamed that they won't tell anyone or instigate legal action, so this bottom-feeding sleaze is still operating.

Beware of dreams with price tags attached. Sleaze merchants prey on the uneducated and those with stars in your eyes. Be pragmatic and know the business; you'll be much safer.

Do Invest Wisely in the Following:

- Publicity and public relations services (including a first-class, professional bio)

- Quality recordings (though keep this in perspective—you don't need 24-track song demos to play for publishers)

- Equipment

- Costumes

- Photos and graphic services

- Your Web site

- Business cards

- Trade magazines

- Dedicated fax machine and phone lines

- A computer

- Musicians. Marta Woodhull, in her ground-breaking book, *Singing for a Living*, suggests that it's always a good idea to pay musicians for their efforts, even if it's not a great deal of money. One reason for this is that it keeps your dealings on a professional level; if someone is doing you a favor by playing for free and happens to be a half hour late to a rehearsal, it's very difficult to give them a hard time for their tardiness. On the other hand, if you're paying them money out of your pocket, even a small amount, you have the necessary leverage to demand a certain degree of professionalism.

- Quality CD duping, mastering, and labeling

Everyone is constantly being sold to. Every hour of radio listening, television watching, and newspaper and magazine reading involves sifting through the various buying opportunities that you encounter. If you create a product or a service, it's essential to know a few basics about how the buying mentality really works.

- For the most part, buyers purchase for two emotional reasons: pride of ownership and prestige. They want to buy.

- Know exactly who your buyer is and their needs. If you're booking an act into a local club, for instance, you know that the bottom line is that the club owner wants to sell drinks. Show that you can make this happen by attracting an audience. Provide recommendations, letters of reference, and referrals to the club owner so they can be assured that you will bring an audience in. If this doesn't work and you know you can pack the club, try offering to perform one night in the club for free. If you can't do what you promise, the club owner doesn't have to pay you—but have the club owner agree to hire you for a couple of weeks if you deliver.

- Know your product inside and out. Product knowledge gives you confidence, and confidence helps you make the sale.

- Don't be afraid to close the sale. If you're trying to give someone a buying opportunity for your services or the services of the act you represent, give them multiple opportunities to say yes. There are as many closes as there are sales approaches, but always ask your closing question in the affirmative, such as, "Is this an opportunity you'd like to take advantage of?"

- Don't give your buyer more than three options. "Would you like us to perform next week or would the week after be better for you?" is a better closing than "Would you like us to play here?"

- No doesn't always mean no—generally, it's only an objection. For every objection, there is an appropriate objection response. Rehearse the sales scenario in your mind and anticipate any objection your buyer may have. Answer the objection directly and go back to the close.

- Successful sales have limited time frames. As buyers, you're probably used to seeing things like "limited time only" special sales. This is a very common device to force a buying decision, or close. A buyer saying, "I want to think about it," is not a good sign, and it diminishes the probability that he will ever buy. Since buyers buy for emotional reasons, keep the energy level high, and make it look like any decision has to be made at the moment it's presented.

- A good salesman assumes the sale will happen; it is already a forgone conclusion. What you're selling is right for the buyer, isn't it? Otherwise, why are you trying to sell him something he doesn't need or want?

The Steak and the Sizzle

It's a well know sales technique that if the buyer buys the credibility of the salesperson, he will generally buy the product the salesman is presenting. Sales doesn't have to be a sleazy, deceptive proposition. It's actually a valuable service.

Although there is a certain aggressive and charismatic personality type who is referred to as a "born salesman," almost anyone can succeed at sales if they understand the basics.

It's essential to be a good listener, because no one likes to be talked at, so actively engage any buyer through dialogue. Both open-ended questions such as, "What type of entertainment do you envision for your event?" and close-ended questions such as, "Do you want blues, reggae, or rock'n'roll?" help you qualify your buyers so you're not wasting your time or theirs.

Never be intimidated by your buyers. Your time is just as important as theirs, so don't sit interminably in their office, allow them to browbeat you, or act over-appreciative for the appointment. Don't attempt to butter up buyers, and don't beat around the bush; get to the point. Always begin by telling the buyer what you're going to sell him. He'll appreciate your honesty, and honesty helps win sales.

REFERRALS

Referrals are the best way to approach someone who doesn't know who you are. If you can use the name of someone your new contact knows and respects, your odds of getting to speak with him will be increased. Never be afraid to ask someone for a referral if you think they'll give you one. However, if you're pitching materials or songs, make sure your contact feels strongly about what you have, otherwise you're putting them in an awkward position by asking for help.

Sometimes it works to use an approach such as, "I'll send it to you to listen to, and if you like it I'd appreciate a referral to Mr. Jones at Acme Records. I know how important your integrity is, and I wouldn't want to put you in a tough position, OK?"

Suppose you need to reach someone and don't have a referral, but you think your odds would be better if you mentioned the name of someone they would instantly recognize. Should you lie just to get through to them?

I would never advise anyone to be less than honest; however, I admit that I did try this one on at least one occasion, and it didn't help. I still didn't get through. In the sales game, many things can unconsciously give you away if you're not being honest. If you've got the goods, you'll get referrals. However, a telephone is not a court of law—you're in business to make money, too. Let your own sense of morals justify your actions. Don't use my name though!

If someone you don't know well offers to refer you to a third party, be sure you understand the relationship between the two. Many times, the way you come in is the way you are perceived. If you've been referred by someone who is not respected, then you in turn will have no respect. I learned this the hard way when I first began managing artists. A contact had referred me to a concert promoter. When I called the promoter and mentioned my contact's name, I was met with an icy silence that I was unsuccessful in defrosting despite my warmest efforts.

The telephone is the single most powerful communications tool ever developed. An artist may spend years developing their instrument, voice, or stage craft. Well, you've got to treat the telephone like an instrument, too, and develop your skills accordingly. Here's how to put it to work for you.

It is absolutely necessary to script what you're going to say on the telephone before you make a call. Your script doesn't have to be word-for-word, but it does have to be outlined. You may have only ten seconds to make a favorable impression—don't blow it by improvising.

Theodore Roosevelt is credited with coining the term "weasel words," meaning, "Words that destroy the force of a statement by equivocal qualification, as a weasel ruins an egg by sucking out its content while leaving it superficially intact." *Might, maybe,* and *perhaps* fall into this category. So do phrases such as, "I just happened to," "I was wondering if," "I think you ought to," and, "Sorry to bother you, but..." These terms instantly show your self- doubt and telegraph your insecurity.

You should always look into a mirror when you're doing any heavy-duty phone calling. Did you know that a smile can be heard on the telephone? Try it sometime when you're talking to a friend. Don't talk *at* people, be responsive to them and learn to listen to what they're saying to you. Receptionists and secretaries can be your allies, so learn their names, don't expect them to educate you, and treat them well.

Sometimes when it's extremely hard to get through to an executive, try calling earlier than the office opens, or about a half-hour after it closes. Many times the support staff leaves, so the exec has to answer his own phone.

The following approach should only be used if you believe you're totally on target, because it can be abrasive. You'll need to rehearse this one. In this example, I'm calling William Jones. I absolutely believe that what I have to say will interest him, but he's hard to get through to.

Receptionist: Acme Records
Me: William Jones, please.

Receptionist: Who shall I say is calling?
Me: Dan Kimpel. May I speak with William Jones, please?

Receptionist: What company are you with?
Me: DKM Management. Would you put me through to William Jones, please?

Receptionist: Will he know what this is regarding?
Me: It's regarding a management client. Will you put me through to William Jones, please?

The point of this approach is not to harass an overworked receptionist; indeed, keep your tone friendly but very strong. It's a rare receptionist who won't back down after being asked four times to put you through. You've got to sound authoritative enough to convince her that you know Mr. Jones, though, and that what you have to say is important to him.

Often, if your phone presence is strong enough, you won't have to go through all of this to get through. Note that it's usually not necessary to tell your whole tale unless you're asked to.

The following example is a more typical scenario

Receptionist: Acme Publishing, good morning
Me: Good morning, this is Dan Kimpel from DKM Management. May I speak with William Jones, please?

Mr. Jones: William Jones.
Me: Good morning, Mr. Jones, this is Dan Kimpel from DKM Management. I'm calling on behalf of a client who has some very strong, accessible R&B material. I know the recent successes your company has had and your role in signing that material, and I'd like to set up a brief appointment to play you three songs this week. Could we meet on Wednesday or Thursday?

At this point, Mr. Jones may grill me further.

Mr. Jones: What type of songs are they?
Me: There's one strong, uptempo dance song [tip: publishers and artists always need uptempo material], a trip-hop mid-tempo tune, and a ballad. We have strong demos, and the publishing is available. Could I come by for a face-to-face this week?

Mr. Jones: Sure, let me give you back to my secretary, and she'll schedule you in.

LEARN THE LANGUAGE

Nothing gives an amateur away like misuse of music business terms. I've heard some dillies: writers who have recorded demos and pronounce it "deemos." Asking "Where do I sell my songs?" is a dead giveaway, because professionals don't "sell" songs—they have them signed, published, or cut, but not sold. "I need an agent or a manager" is another dead giveaway because these are totally separate functions. To learn the language of music, it's essential to hang around with the people who speak it.

Musicians

To the uninitiated, the arcane language of professional musicians can sound like a foreign tongue, punctuated by the word "man" at least once per sentence. There is a musician-speak that could be the subject of a whole other book. Musicians generally like to talk about their gear (that is, equipment). Learning about the various instruments and having strong opinions about them is a good opener; talk vintage guitars and you can't lose. Keyboard players tend to be tech heads, so know enough about the cutting-edge developments to sound knowledgeable. Never be afraid to ask a musician his opinion about instruments, or music for that matter; odds are they'll love to tell you.

Musicians are clannish; they can be very standoffish and insular. I've seen them be brutal to singers in a studio situation who didn't know how to ask for what they wanted. Some rudimentary music courses can be very helpful in assisting you to communicate with musicians who may be in your network or employ. A tip: never refer to any musical sound as a "noise."

Songwriters

To talk to songwriters, you'll need to be conversant about the parts of a song. Know what a verse, bridge, and chorus are. Know rhyme scheme terminology like AABB, ABAB. Know that songs are written, not "made up." Know about the demos and enough about the technology to get what you want in the studio. Know the terminology of the publishing business, what a "hold" is, what a copublishing deal is, what actually happens when a publisher likes your song.

The book I mentioned earlier, *The Craft and Business of Songwriting* by John Braheny, is a great place to begin to learn the songwriting language. Becoming affiliated with a local or national songwriter organization will put you in contact with other songwriters.

Within the Business

Know what a record deal, a spec deal, a publishing deal, points, and recording fund are. Know enough musician-speak to be able to communicate, the same with recording studio jargon. You should begin learning about recording consoles, digital recording, analog tape machines, and outboard equipment. The best way to learn is by asking questions of those around you who know. Engineers and producers are generally very enthusiastic about discussing equipment.

When I interviewed Donald Passman in Chapter Three of this book, I was sitting in his office after the session talking about my management business. I said to him that I had taken courses at UCLA when I started in the business because I didn't know everything I thought I should know. Donald replied that when you get into a new endeavor in the music business, it's not necessary to know everything off the bat and in fact, it's not necessarily an advantage. How you learn what you know through your experiences and how you ultimately use this knowledge to become more effective is much more important.

It has been said that there are no stupid questions. When I'm not exactly sure of what is being discussed (say with my client's record company), and I need to understand thoroughly, I'll preface a query with this gem of verbalese that I learned from a lawyer friend: "In the interest of absolute clarity..."

Learning the language will become second nature to you. Be a sponge: read every book and periodical that you can about the business and attend seminars, classes, and training sessions, but most of all be around people who are doing what you want to do. The language will become instinctive and natural.

Hooples

When I lived in New York City, I performed regularly at a nightclub on Bleecker Street called the Back Fence. A Greenwich Village institution, the joint was run by two crusty brothers named Ernie and Rocky Scinto who spoke an intriguing and exotic New Yorkese that included the word "hoople." The first time I heard them use this word and asked what it meant they looked at me as only New Yorkers can and replied, "Just what it sounds like." In the music business, hooples are people who call you up and, at the expense of your time, expect you to accommodate, facilitate, and educate them. They don't know the first thing about the business or how it works. These people are time-wasters.

I pride myself on being very accessible. It's unfortunate when I encounter individuals who make me want to bar my open door. They are hooples. Hooples are instantly identifiable—to avoid being one, follow these guidelines:

Do This on the Phone

- Script your call.

- Be honest.

- Get right to the point.

- Sound friendly.

- Use the person's name you're speaking to at least once a minute.

- Be very courteous.

- Have a lot of energy!

- Sound intelligent.

- Turn off your call waiting on your phone.

- Learn the language.

- Let them know who referred you to them.

- Show that you've done research about their company or services.

- Show that you're listening to them by repeating what they've said to you or echoing their key points.

- Be positive.

Good Opening Lines

- "Here's exactly why I'm calling..."

- "Let me get right to the point..."

- "Here's the situation..."

- "I'm sure you're busy, but I wanted to communicate a quick idea."

Don't Do This (Instant Hoopledom!)

- Begin a conversation by saying, "Hello, who is this?"

- Take more than ten seconds to get to the point.

- Say "um," or hem and haw.

- Have a television on (it makes me crazy to get a call from someone at "XYZ Productions" who is attempting to big-time me on the phone and I can hear their television and a wailing baby in the background). Silence, please.

- Say "Let me get a pencil." Don't pick up the phone unless you're prepared to write!

- Eat or chew gum.

- Yawn.

- Use a cheap phone.

- Talk too softly or too loudly.

- Lay your lips on the phone.

- Use a speaker phone.

- Lie.

- Mispronounce a name.

- Talk too long.

- Begin your conversation with "How are you?" This is a cliché. Do you really care?

- Cop an attitude.

    It's essential that you speak with authority and sound dynamic. Since people generally appreciate the entertainment value of all communications, keep in mind that you have to hold their attention by sounding interesting in order to make them receptive to anything you may have to say. There's a phrase popular in L.A.: "gives good phone." It refers to someone who knows exactly how to use the instrument and whose calls you actually look forward to receiving. They're people who are entertaining, fun, energetic, and always have something to say. They respect your time, they respect their own, and they can get the job done.

THE BASICS OF NETWORKING BY PHONE

1. Set aside specific hours to make calls. You really have to be up to be successful on the phone, so figure out the specific time slot you can be at your verbal best. For me, it's around 11 AM.

2. Try to make most of your calls before lunch.

3. Remember that it's hard to find music people in their offices on Monday and Friday.

4. Configure an "A" calling list (once a week) of your closest contacts, a "B" list of people to call once a month, and a "C" list for six month intervals.

5. *Never call someone without something specific to say!*

6. If you're calling to tout your own accomplishments, always begin by focusing on your contact. "I saw an article today that made me think of you." "I was wondering how you were progressing with..." Just calling to touch base is not a reason to call important contacts.

7. Anytime you see anything of note having to do with your network, you have a perfect opportunity to call, as well as an opening. "I saw an article..." or, "I see you have a song on the new XXX album"—even a club listing for a local band will do. Read everything having to do with your network, especially local music columns, club listings, and wedding and birth notices. Look at the list of fictitious business announcements (DBAs) in your local paper to see if any music-related businesses have opened their doors.

8. Make all of your calls short, sweet, and to the point.

9. Start by indicating that your call is going to be a brief one. Saying, "I know you're busy, so I'll keep his short" is a good way to prepare your listener and allow him to relax, knowing that you're not going to keep him on the phone all day. "I have three things to discuss with you" lets your listener know what to anticipate and that you're organized and professional.

10. Make notes that you can refer to on your next go-around, such as, "How's that demo going that we discussed?" "How was your gig at the X club?" Don't make it obvious that you're reading off of notes; make your contact think that the information he told you a week, a month, or even six months ago, was important enough for you to remember.

11. Never be afraid to pick up the phone to call someone. Prepare, think what you want to say, and go for it. I know how difficult this can be, but I also know how necessary it is. Remember, no one can reach out and grab and shake you over the phone. Be sensitive enough to your listener to know when they're busy or not into the conversation, but you've got to reach out.

12. If you call someone, it's your responsibility to end the call, always.

13. Never take a call on another line, then return to your original caller and announce how important the call on the other line is. This is very bad form.

14. Listen to not just the words, but to the emotions and sensitivity behind them.

Rolodexes/Phone Files

Invest in a good Rolodex or card file. It's not necessary to type the names. In fact, it's easier if you don't, because you can change them more easily to keep track of your list of contacts and your networking prospects. When using a computer, use a database form that's easy to use and has enough room to make notes—and back it up often.

Legal pads are good tracking devices, too; I use them constantly for all of my contacts to transcribe raw information. I keep all of the pads and have been surprised how many times they've saved me when I had to refer back to information I thought I'd transferred to a more suitable location.

CORRESPONDENCE

It's an old adage that the written word has more credibility that a phone call. The rule of thumb in correspondence is brevity. Never write more than one page about anything if you expect a busy person to read it. If you don't have a computer, you should certainly think about making this vital investment as soon as possible. If you plan on generating large quantities of written materials, a computer is a must. You can program your basic letter and then alter it to meet specific situations so you won't have to rewrite it each time and still keep your submissions relatively uniform.

Good looking stationery, preferably with your own letterhead and matching envelopes, shows the recipient that you mean business.

The following letter to Lou Jeffries is an example of letters I've written when submitting tapes and press kits to contacts on behalf of my management clients (I've changed the name and addresses here in the interest of privacy). Notice that I let the recipient know where we met, thanked him for his help, let him know he requested the information, and used a casual, informal close.

February 20, 2000

Lou Jeffries
923 S. Clark Dr.
Beverly Hills, CA 90211

Dear Lou,

I enjoyed meeting you at the video shoot at Descano Gardens on Friday. Thanks for your insight—the information will be helpful in putting together my article.

Find enclosed the tape on my management client that you requested. I've also enclosed some recent press and bio information.

 Enjoy the CD. Thanks for your interest, Lou.

Warmest Regards,

Dan Kimpel
DKM MANAGEMENT

Say Thanks Often and Honestly

A thank-you note is the single most effective piece of writing you can send to someone. Believe me, it appeals to everyone to be thanked, honestly and sincerely, for what they've done. The following is a thank you letter I sent to a second engineer who went above and beyond the call of duty on a recent marathon recording session. (Note: I enclosed this note with a box of chocolate-covered macadamia nuts. Do you think he'll remember me?)

May 12, 2000

Bob Leeds
Eastlake Recording
211 Beverly Blvd.
Hollywood, CA 90093

Dear Bob,

Just a brief note to thank you for the energy and enthusiasm you lent to last week's session. We certainly couldn't have completed the tracks or achieved the sound without your help.

I'll look forward to working with you soon; please feel free to use me as a reference for any prospective clients.

Sincerely,

Dan Kimpel

Postcards

There is no cheaper way to communicate than the lowly postcard. Postcards can be wonderful little reminders that you're thinking of someone, and often the funnier or more bizarre they are, the better. It's a rare trip that I take home to Lima, Ohio, that I don't pick up a stack of unlikely looking postcards with such lovely pictures as the local oil refinery, a K-Mart parking lot, or the Lima Mall. People remember these slices of Americana I send, and I always get amused comments from them.

A friend in PR suggests having a stack of postcards already stamped on your desk to send out to networking acquaintances. Don't think about it, just do it.

Cold Contact Letters

Some songwriters and artists prepare fairly elaborate response cards to inquire about music business submissions. Response cards are preprinted postcards that are enclosed with inquiry letters sent to music publishers and record companies to find out about their material submission policies. They ask:

- If the company is accepting material

- How many songs to send

- What type of material is needed

- What format to send (lately, CD is the standard)

- If material will be returned if you provide a SASE (self-addressed, stamped envelope)

Although this may help some songwriters or artists to find out about the possibility of sending unsolicited material, it's been my observation that a properly used telephone is generally more expedient. Always contact the company to find out the name pronunciation, spelling, and exact title of the appropriate person who listens to incoming submissions. Writing a letter to "Attention A&R" or "Professional Manager" is the work of an amateur, so know the person's name.

Since I believe in networking as the most viable way into the music business, I don't believe that blindly sending out tapes to record companies is the best way to advance your career. You need personal contacts. The best way to begin your search through the maze of record and publishing companies is by using *Songwriters Market, A&R 411,* or *The Recording Industry Source Book* (see "Resources" for more information).

Always send follow-up letters to contacts as soon as possible. Don't delay, especially if you've just met someone and they want to hear your tape, CD, or other materials. As you're probably aware, most people have remarkably short attention spans and memories, so send a letter the week you've met someone, and follow up the letter with a call (or a fax) as soon as you're sure they've had ample time to listen to your tape (probably within another week). When you call, remind them again of what you've sent, because you may be helping them out of a potentially embarrassing situation. Your window of contact only stays open for a certain period of time. Calling someone six months down the road who you met briefly on one occasion may make them question your motives. Contacting them within a shorter period of time is more natural.

Just the Fax

Faxes walk a fine line between telephone calls and the written word. They are valuable tools for following up other types of communication, especially telephone calls, but they do not possess the weight of a letter. Often it is easier to get through with a fax than a call, because the recipient isn't required to immediately respond and can read a communiqué at their leisure.

Plain-paper faxes are preferable, since they eliminate the crinkled curled look of thermal fax paper. Fax machines are a notoriously unstable medium—the paper often jams or simply runs out on the roll. For this reason, it is always necessary—when important information is being transmitted—to follow-up a fax with a telephone call.

Many computers now send and receive faxes with ease. This alleviates the above physical limitations.

E-mail

E-mail is a wonderful, low-cost way to communicate with a wide network of contacts. It is widely used in the business world—not only for interoffice communications, but also for intraoffice contact—that is, within companies. E-mail allows for synchronous communication—conversations that are not in real time. I find e-mail particularly useful for overseas communication to locales where the cost of telephone calls would be prohibitive.

It is often much easier for me to respond to e-mail than to either a telephone call or a letter, and I prefer it for queries, questions, and comments. However, e-mail does not possess the weight of the written word and—for better or worse—can be ignored.

A word about *spamming:* If you have e-mail, you have no doubt been subjected to unwanted messages. Generally these can be detected and deleted without having to read them.

I find it annoying when people within my e-mail network send me platitudes, treacly inspirational stories, or tasteless jokes. I do not recommend sending any of these to a contact whom you are not 100 percent sure would appreciate them.

For press releases, e-mails are valuable, but again, they do not have the power of a letter. If you use e-mail to publicize your events, I recommend that you use it as a supplemental medium, not as your only method.

THE NAME GAME

Everyone likes to have his or her name pronounced and spelled correctly as well as remembered. When you meet people in a networking situation, it's important to instantly commit their name to memory. Repetition is the key here; say their name at least three times in the conversation. Keep a small notepad in your possession and makes notes, surreptitiously if you can. That way you know exactly who you've encountered and when. Never be afraid to ask someone for a business card, but be aware of subtle and not-so-subtle signs. I've seen A&R people and publishers claim that they're "fresh out." This usually means a temporarily closed door for the aspirant. I once watched a record company executive walk through a music industry convention with his name-bearing badge turned around, so no one would know who he was and attempt to engage him in dialogue or give him tapes.

When you write to someone, it's important to know their title. Don't trust your resource materials 100 percent. If you're submitting to a record company, a publisher, or the media, call and ask the receptionist the exact title. Titles are subject to change, and sending something to Bill Jones, A&R Manager when it should be Bill Jones, Vice President of A&R, will create a negative impression. You want the recipients of your efforts to know that you're aware of their position in the company.

BUSINESS CARDS

A great-looking business card is a pretty good investment. The availability of computers and laser printers make designing your own card fairly easy, and print shops also have facilities and professional expertise. Make sure your card is very readable by avoiding bizarre or limiting type styles, and keep it very simple. When you move or change phone numbers, get new cards. Don't cross out the old phone number and continue to use the card; it's tacky and amateurish. Avoid clichés in your description of what you do, and don't attempt to consolidate too many of your various identities on one card.

If you wear more than one hat, get more than one business card; it won't break the bank.

You will also want to avoid tacky clip art that hasn't changed since the 1950s. Tired-looking music notes and spinning records fall into this category. Look at the type styles and designs in current magazines. Cut out the type styles and graphics you think would be suitable for you, and use these as examples to emulate or show to your typesetter.

Keep your business cards in a holder designed for this purpose; that way, they won't get dog-eared and will be easily accessible.

COMMUNICATING WITH THE PRESS

The press is a valuable ally. Learn the art of communicating with them via well-written press releases.

The Calendar Listing

The calendar listing gives just the who, what, when, and why. In the market I work, this has to be received at least three weeks in advance of the event. This information must be sent directly to the individual who is responsible for compiling, editing, and placing it in the publication, the calendar editor. Find out the name and title of this person by calling the publication.

The following is an example of material you would send to the calendar editor.

JULY 31 FOR IMMEDIATE RELEASE
CONTACT: Dan Kimpel, (213) 555-1212

WHO: Luis Villegas
WHAT: Latin guitar virtuoso with his band, The U.N.
WHERE: Sunset Junction Street Fair, at the intersection of
Sunset and Santa Monica Boulevards, Los Angeles
WHEN: Saturday, August 21, 5:00 PM
WHY: Sunset Junction Street Fair, August 21 and 22, is a
vibrant street festival celebrating the diversity of the
surrounding neighborhood through music, dance, art, crafts,
and food.

BACKGROUND:
Luis Villegas' brand of Latin music is equal parts finger-shred-
ding arpeggios, infectious rhythms, languid, hypnotic jams,
and intricate, unforgettable melodies. His band percolates with
passion and percussion while Luis' virtuoso guitar floats high
above the fire. Villegas will be performing selections from his
Domo Records debut, *Cafe Olé*.

The Press Release

A press release is written in a more literary and descriptive
style than a calendar listing announcement. It also incorporates the who, what, when, where, and why, but in addition it
should also give the probably harassed editor at the local paper
an angle on the event. It's been my experience that many
times the press release becomes the article, so make it as
complete as possible. Direct your releases to the appropriate
contact; don't send the news editor an entertainment release,
for example. Then call the appropriate department to make
sure that the information was received. If your contact claims
they didn't receive it, be prepared to resend or fax the information again.

The way to interest the press is to create newsworthy events for
them to cover. "Band plays club, ten people come and drink" is
not worthy of press attention. You've got to think about their
needs, not just yours.

Memorize the differences between the following categories.

ADVERTISING: the purchase of space in a paper or magazine to let readers know about an event, product, or service.

PUBLICITY: hard news coverage occurring before the event. Is there a newsworthy aspect (for example, is this the first event of its kind? Is it the only one?) that will help get coverage?

PROMOTION: putting up flyers, posters, sending direct mail.

PUBLIC RELATIONS: a response to your event in the form of a story through the eyes, pen, or camera of an electronic or print journalist.

In order to pitch the media on your event, band or service you've got to write a short pitch letter, send a complete and professional press kit and make sure that you're targeting the proper outlet for the information.

The following is an examples of a press release written for the same event as the previous calendar listing example.

CONTACT: DAN KIMPEL (213) 555-1212

July 31 FOR IMMEDIATE RELEASE

<u>LUIS VILLEGAS</u>
<u>TAKES CENTER STAGE</u>
<u>AT SUNSET JUNCTION</u>

It will be a welcome homecoming when **Luis Villegas** returns to his old neighborhood to perform at the **Sunset Junction Street Fair** on **Saturday, August 21**.

This past year saw the release of **Villegas'** major label debut, *Cafe Olé,* a series of national tour dates, and inclusion in a number of films including *Lost & Found* staring **David Spade** (Warner Bros.). **Villegas** wrote two songs for the film and one of the tunes, **"Banana Bay"** is featured on the **Capitol Records** soundtrack.

Villegas, born in East Los Angeles, grew up near the site of the festival. He began playing guitar in the Sunset Strip's smoky rock dens but returned to his roots and the traditional nylon-string guitar. Though **Villegas** retains a rock zeal is his playing, his emerging maturity has taught him to speak in many musical languages, both as an instrumentalist and as a composer.

With his debut album, **Villegas** has garnered rave reviews, new fans, and national recognition. He will bring it all back home to the Edgecliff Stage at 5:00 p.m. on Saturday.

# # #

The Bio

The addition of a bio can certainly make your pitch to the press much stronger. The following is an example of a bio that I wrote for a client. He uses this material as a part of his press kit. I also developed an edited "one-sheet" that uses key paragraphs and is sent out to program directors of radio stations and magazines along with his record.

HAROLD PAYNE PASSES IT ON

100 years ago, Harold Payne would have jumped freight trains or stowed away on tramp steamers. He could have written novels like Jack London, painted portraits of exotic native womanhood like Paul Gauguin, and been a guide through steaming jungles from the farthest outposts of known civilization.

In these days of the jet plane, Harold Payne uses songs, his voice, and a guitar to traverse a global road that has led him from Chiang Mai to Moscow, from Bali to Bora-Bora. He's worked on film scores in India, toured Japan, and appeared as a regular on Australian television. He's sung in Singapore, he's strummed in Samoa, he's dreamt in Hindu temples, and jammed with the itinerant street musicians of Ireland: he shares it with us on his new Affinity Records release *Pass It On*.

Harold Payne's global orientation came to him naturally as he grew up in the multicultural melting pot of Gardena, California. Growing up with Japanese, Hawaiian, African-American, and Mexican neighbors allowed Harold an intimate glimpse into other cultures and the opportunity to experience a broad geographical spectrum of music.

On the homefront, Payne's songs have garnered over 100 cover versions for other artists. His song "I Wish He Didn't Trust Me So Much" reached the #2 spot on the Billboard R&B charts for Bobby Womack, and singers from Patti Labelle to the Cover Girls have brought Harold's songs to the public via radio and record mediums. Motion pictures *Beverly Hills Cop II*, *Splash*, and *Summer Rental* are just a few of the films with which Harold has been involved musically. His group Gravity has toured to support their successful album release in Japan, and Harold cowrote "Music Speaks Louder Than Words," the theme song for a Songwriter Summit held in the former Soviet Union, where Payne and top songwriters, including Cyndi Lauper, Brenda Russell, Michael Bolton, and Barry Mann, met in a spirit of international harmony with their Soviet counterparts.

Though Harold Payne has performed for audiences of 10,000 plus, opening shows for Kenny Loggins, Van Morrison, and Heart, his sterling musicianship and one-on-one communication are apparent in any given setting: concerts, clubs, or coffeehouses. Whether with a band or solo, Payne's gift for improvisation and instinctive rapport with a audience have been honed by a lifetime of being onstage, using the rhythm of his music to provide a continuing physical bridge to a diverse and involved group of listeners.

"Half a world apart, there's no space between our hearts," sings Harold Payne on this intensely personal yet immediately accessible album, *Pass it On*. A rich and sophisticated musical patina paints the sound with acoustic guitars, choral vocal harmonies, and sparkling synthesizers, providing the frame for Payne's husky heartfelt vocals. The songs on this collection, recorded with different producers in various studios in Los Angeles, are unified through the songwriting. In the world of Harold Payne, the songs are the most important element ("The song is king," he states simply), and the ten selections on *Pass it On* are so genuine and natural they sound as if they may have written themselves. The chance encounter, the moment that might have been, the distances between lovers physical and emotional, and the solitary view where the city lights recede from the window of an airplane and blend into the stars over a dark ocean, are all here.

So Harold Payne continues: to write, to celebrate, to travel, to perform, and to make a musical difference. The positivity of his music is bound to affect audiences, whether they're longtime fans or brand new listeners. "We can make a difference…a single candle in the night can turn the darkness into light," he sings, and by allowing us to share his artistry, he lets us commune with that warmth and to experience the power of his singular musical vision.

###

This bio works because Harold Payne's music is actually as interesting as I described it. He'd had other press kit items written for him that he didn't like because they were too exclusive. Notice that as flattering as the descriptions are, I didn't use superlatives: They have no place in press materials.

Which Media to Use When

If you don't have a record out, don't bother trying to place stories in the national media. It does absolutely no good to have a story in a high profile medium if there's not an item for the reader to purchase; it's a waste of time and energy. Save major press for when you have a record to promote.

Only use the local media when you have an event that readers can go to or a product that they can purchase easily and, preferably, as soon as they read about it! Keep in mind that in our media-inundated society, the more sources you can use to imprint your information on the general public, the better. It often takes at least three separate sources of information to make a lasting impact on someone, and even then, they may not know where they got the information.

If you're going to pitch the media on your projects, make sure you've got the right person on the line. The entertainment editor is your surest bet and is probably someone who actually has an office at the publication. Many times, freelancers or contributing editors work out of their homes for more than one publication. Receptionists will freely give you this information if you use the telephone techniques described in this chapter to sound authoritative. If you invite the media to an event, notify them of it in ample time, make the event sound as interesting as possible, and follow up the week before the event. You can check to see if the materials you sent arrived and verbally reinforce your pitch. The offices of many major magazines resemble Auntie Em's farm after the tornado, so materials are easily misplaced or misfiled. Know the type of person you're dealing with, and be prepared to do the thinking for them; they may not know where your project falls in terms of how to cover it. Tell them. Have confidence and enthusiasm, and keep in mind that timing is of the essence.

Stories can fall into place in ways you might not imagine. I recently pitched a client to a magazine that agreed, rather disinterestedly, that they'd do "something." Two days before their scheduled deadline, their cover story interview fell through, so the small story they'd anticipated writing about my client was now on the cover. They had to scramble to interview him by phone, but we had much more space in the magazine than we'd ever expected.

IF YOU WANT SOMETHING DONE RIGHT, DO IT YOURSELF

In promoting upcoming shows, events, and gigs, never rely on anyone, even a reputable public relations firm, to do your work for you. This was illustrated to me recently when I received a fax from a PR firm concerning a multiartist outdoor concert with one of my acts on the bill. The PR agency sent me a fax of a memo they'd received from the promoter of the show that instructed them to provide bios and pictures to the press, but my act wasn't one of the ones designated to receive this special attention.

However, I'd already serviced the press with the show information, featuring my act's bio, picture, and a media-ready press release. Every music magazine in Southern California already had this information, and it was sent well in advance of the show, since I knew each publication's lead time, with my act listed first. I had also made friends within the PR agency and let them understand that I was there to work with them in the promotion of my act and the overall event. (I doubt if any of the other act's management companies had ingratiated themselves in this way.) Consequently, my act received the greatest amount of advance press for the event and appeared to be the headliner, even if the promoter didn't necessarily see it that way.

From this, I was able to add the PR firm to my network, and, by also using my preexistent press network to get me coverage for my act, we were able to make the show's press a major coup.

Here's another example of why you shouldn't rely on anyone else to get the job done. I have a friend who was on the road as the tour coordinator with a mid-level urban act. They were performing in Philadelphia, and she'd sent a fax to the promoter that clearly showed the time that their entourage would be arriving at the airport, how many were in their party, how large a limo they needed, and how big a passenger and equipment van for the musicians and crew. After sending the fax, she followed up by calling the promoter to make sure he'd received it. He assured her he had. The next day, when the 20-person entourage arrived at the airport, there was no one there to meet them, and the star was livid. When the tour manager called the promoter, he admitted that he had received the fax but neglected to read it, even though the act was arriving the next day! That's rock'n'roll. My friend kept her job, barely, but she learned a valuable lesson.

Musicians will be late, trucks will be towed away, flyers won't be ready on time, names will be misspelled, mics will fall on the floor, and the promoter will owe you money. Such is the way of the music world. Rather than allowing this to depress you, even momentarily, anticipate disasters, but don't overanticipate. Have enough confidence in your own abilities to work and make correct instinctive decisions under pressure so that you'll be ready for whatever may occur in the line of fire, because that's the reality of this business.

THE THIS-REALLY-HAPPENED DEPARTMENT

I sent a press kit and tape on a client to a specialized local magazine in Los Angeles. When I called the next week, I asked for the editor to whom I'd sent the materials. The receptionist was very guarded and said he wasn't there. when I asked when he'd be in, she said "Do you know him?" When I admitted I didn't, she let loose with this information: "He died last week. Is there anyone else who can help you?" My first impulse was to try to make light of this, but my inner critic thankfully prevailed and I could only whisper, "I'm so sorry." I was referred to another editor (his successor) and actually ended up getting a cover story for my client. Be prepared for this sort of unexpected situation—not just deaths, but firings, promotions, transfers, etc.

YOU CAN LEAD A JOURNALIST TO WATER...

When I began doing public relations for clients, I learned one lesson fast. One of my first clients was an author/educator who had just published a book. I contacted the media, sent out press releases and press copies, and got reviews in a number of magazines. The only problem is that not all of the magazines felt as positively about the book as others and, in fact, one of the reviews was downright evil.

Fortunately, my client and I, throughout two separate lifetimes in the entertainment industry, have developed the emotions of zombies when it comes to the criticism of our work. I suggest that you do the same if you're going to be involved in public relations and promotion of events. Critics are paid to offer their opinions, and not everyone is going to like what they see. Our goals as creative people should never be to please all of the people all of the time, because that means that we're rounding off all of the edges on our work simply to appease popular tastes. In the culinary world, when you do this you create a bland, processed hamburger. In the music business, you create bland, processed elevator music.

Don't worry too much about bad press. Negative reviews have a way of leaving the mind of the reader, and often what they remember is the name of the product, not one writer's negative opinion of it.

WRAP-UP

Sales, persuasion, public relations, and hype are not dirty words. They are necessary ingredients in the positive development of your career and in your life. It is essential that you have enough self-awareness to realize which of your traits is most salable. You may have to step outside of yourself to see that if you're banging your head against a rock maybe it's time to walk around it and to pursue things in a new adventurous way and chart your own course.

Belief is the strongest selling point of all, so only commit yourself to what you truly believe in, dig in for a long haul, and use every power you can conjure up to convince others that you're right. Use your imagination, and trust your instincts and perceptions.

Putting it All Together

s you've been reading this book, you've probably been able to come up with ideas for applying the information I've given you to your own career. As I've mentioned, there is no standard set of rules for doing things in the music industry. Only guidelines can be provided, and it's up to you to make them work for you.

The following is a personal checklist: Assess yourself as honestly as you can when considering these questions.

FOR PERFORMERS AND SONGWRITERS

1. *Is your career the most important thing in your life?*
As we've discussed throughout this book, the individuals who are successful as performers in the music business all share a single-minded resolve and commitment to their music. Is your resolve exemplified through your single-minded devotion to your career?

2. *Are you unique enough to succeed?*
In the music business, performers are defined by what they create, so it's essential that the image presented to a potential audience is a unique one. Yes, the music business is always looking for "the next big thing," but they may not know it when they see it. It's up to you to define your image through music, video, performance, fashion, and a unique statement.

3. *Is your music honestly better than what is currently available on record?*
Your music has to be unique. Recreating something that already exists may provide you with a living in clubs, but it won't help you to convince a record company that there is an untapped market for your music. You have to let the music from your imagination and heart connect with people who will accept, understand, and market it.

4. *Can you explain who your audience is?*
Even though you're unique, you've got to be able to define what radio stations will play your music and expose you to an audience of buyers. The baby boomers whose numbers and buying power made the record business what it is don't currently buy much new rock product; so billions of dollars of CD technology was utilized to rerecord the hits of the 1960s and '70s to sell to this audience. The current fascination with MP3 files and online buying will provide yet another boom. The current explosion in country music can also be attributed to older buyers who are alienated from hard rock and rap music because country, with it's rock edge, is a logical choice for these listeners.

The return of the "boy bands" is related to the children of the baby boom. Buying patterns in music reflect these demographic bumps.

World and ambient music are providing outlets for creative artists who previously wouldn't have fit into a preexisting format. College radio has been instrumental in breaking more radical bands for teenagers, still the largest buyers of prerecorded music.

5. *(Performers) Is your audience a record-buying one?*
This relates to our previous point: record companies are in the business of selling records, period. Fortunately for artists who may not fit into traditional formats, there is alternative marketing; Web-based, mail order, and point-of-purchase concert sales can help an act generate revenue and credibility while climbing the ladder to success. These avenues will be significant in proving to a label that there is a market for your music.

6. *(Performers) Are you young enough to have a long career in the music industry?*
Many of the acts being signed today are in their teens and early 20s, as has always been the case with popular music. A young audience identifies with young performers. Even though there are older bands who tour and record successfully, their audience has grown up with them. In the history of show business, many performers have altered their ages downward to give them an edge in appealing to a younger market. One reason that record companies may be reluctant to sign an older artist is the perception that he has already fulfilled his growth cycle, so the input that he receives from producers,

A&R, etc., won't have much impact on his music; he has finished developing. Bands and performers who are younger will always have an advantage when it comes to getting signed, but there have always been and will always be exceptions to this rule. It's gratifying when talent and hard work win out to expose a new, though not so young, artist.

7. (Performers) Does the individuality of your looks qualify you for video stardom?

Videos have put the faces of artists in front of millions of people. Because rock'n'roll has always been more about individuality of looks rather than glamour, performers have to invent styles that fit with their music. A performer should learn about movement and motion in order to present his best visual image to the cameras.

8. Are you investing enough of your income into your career?

You are responsible for investing in your success. You need demos; if you're a performer, you'll need pictures, press kits, videos, and costumes. You may need to pay musicians or publicists; you need to be resourceful in making your money stretch as far as possible. As we discussed in the previous chapter, bartering can help you to achieve your goals, but seed money is necessary to start any business.

9. Do others share your enthusiasm?

We, as creative people, can't operate in a vacuum. We require inspiration from those around us. If you're not getting this from your current network, you either need to expand it, or to devote your energies to making music that reaches more people, particularly those who can add their energies to your project.

10. Can you generate loyalty in others?

You need support from a network; you will need to inspire others to stay with you through your growth period and through the potentially lean economic times. Let those whom you trust and respect influence you with their artistic input into your project. The best possible way to convince others to be loyal to you is by being loyal to them and encouraging their efforts.

11. (Performers) Can you make audiences crazy?
Rock'n'roll is a kinetic experience where performers and audience merge. Country music performers are often singers whom the audience can imagine sitting down and drinking a beer with after the show. Other forms of music may explore the relationship between audience and performer a little differently, but audiences certainly have to respond to what you do in order for you to be successful.

Most record companies need to see performers live before signing them. Therefore, the chemistry that you create on stage is vital to your success as an artist, particularly in rock-'n'roll and country music. You have to pay some dues and work in front of audiences as often as possible to learn what you do best to connect with them. Do whatever is necessary to make them respond to you; use your imagination. This is show business.

12. Are you experiencing artistic growth?
Creative people need to change and evolve. Open yourself up to new influences, musically, visually, and conceptually. Try new things, talk to different people, work with different cowriters and musicians. Don't get in a rut.

13. Are you actively involved in the study of dance, voice, or song-writing?
Expanding and honing your abilities is rewarding, not only in your career, but also in your life. If you're in a location where you don't have access to classes or workshops, can you create informal ones with your networking contacts? Informal song-writing workshops can be very stimulating; they will also give you one of the key motivational reasons to create: you'll have an outlet.

14. Do you read books that can educate you about your career?
We are fortunate to live in an era when information about the music business is readily accessible. Make a list of books to read; buy them, borrow them, or convince your local library to order them for you and any other aspiring reader who will learn from reading them.

15. *Do you work at achieving maximum outreach, by calling managers, publishers, agents, etc.?*

Sometimes it's difficult to motivate yourself to make the calls and meet the people you need to meet. If you're using a goal list, as discussed in Chapter Four, isolate a specific time for outreach. Write down the calls to be made each week and religiously apply yourself to completing this list.

16. *Does everyone on the local level know who you are?*

You have to lay your groundwork locally before you can be successful nationally and globally. Don't let the light of future success blind you to helpful folks around you; they can lead you to their contacts and help you to expand your network. Don't be jealous of successful performers in your hometown; network with them and use their success to expand your own network.

17. *Do you need to relocate to another city to be successful?*

If you need to do it, do it. Plan, research, and visit first, though, because the more contacts you have the better. Be realistic with your time goals in your chosen city; you won't experience overnight success. Also, take advantage of the fact that you can now reinvent yourself.

18. *Are you afraid of succeeding?*

Fear of success shows itself in many ways, but mostly through you not doing what you know you need to do. Trust your instincts. One prominent Grand Dame dance mistress, when asked by young dancers if they should pursue a full-time career in dance, would invariably answer "no." She determined that if they had to ask her, then they hadn't made up their own minds; therefore, they didn't have the necessary ambition or confidence in their abilities to succeed.

19. *Are you consciously or unconsciously sabotaging your career?*

You can sabotage yourself in obvious or subtle ways with the same result. By not doing what you know you need to do, working with negative and unsupportive people, using drugs and alcohol, allowing yourself to be separated from your music, prostituting your talents, or getting in a rut, you telegraph to others that you don't want to be successful.

1. *Are you doing everything possible to educate yourself about this business?*

Volunteering or interning, reading, studying *Billboard* magazine, and taking classes are just a few of the ways to learn more about the business. Also, going out and hearing music as often as possible, meeting the people who create it locally, and finding your niche should be your priorities.

2. *Do you have the financial resources to direct into your career?*

Just as the potential hit recording artist needs to invest in himself, so do you. The more you have to offer to members of your network, the more valuable you'll be. Having a good piece of equipment, a video camera, a photo studio, or a computer will give you bartering leverage.

3. *Can you hear the hits?*

If you're going to manage bands or work in administrative support capacity, you have to have a clear instinct about what makes a band or performer viable in the marketplace. Try listening to new records and predicting which ones will be in the Top 10. Listen carefully to establish the patterns shared by the top records such as the writing, production, musicianship, and subject matter.

4. *Do you have vision?*

Are you able to envision your success and share that vision with others? Successful managers can work with their acts to develop long term plans. It's impossible to see into the future, but creating goals can help to shape it.

5. *Are you an active or a reactive person?*

Active people take action, create scenarios, have plans, and are aggressive. Reactive people respond to the opportunities placed before them. Most successful music business entrepreneurs are active people.

6. *Can you direct others to do what you need?*

You need to be forceful enough to command others and charismatic enough that they'll want to do what you want. If they like you, respect you, and trust your judgment, this will be relatively simple.

7. Are you a good salesperson?
As discussed in Chapter Five, sales can determine your success. Devote your attention to this function; your ability to sell can give you an in to the business. Often, in a creative scene, there may be a glut of creative talent and a shortage of people who know how to present and sell it.

8. Do you present yourself effectively?
Clothes, physical bearing, and social skills all telegraph who you are to others before you say a word. Look and act the part of a music industry professional; observe those around you who are successful in this business. What traits do they share that you have or can develop?

9. Are your verbal skills representative of your intellect?
The words that we use in conversation are one of the primary ways that we're judged. Listen to yourself in conversation. Do you use too much slang or profanity? You can expand your word usage by using a thesaurus or dictionary and by writing down interesting and descriptive words from magazines and newspapers and then adding them to your vocabulary.

10. Are your writing skills up to par?
A writing class in high school or college can be invaluable in later life. Computer skills are a prerequisite in the current marketplace, but knowing *what* to write is certainly as important as knowing how. Familiarize yourself with standard business letters, practice writing press releases and bios as shown in Chapter Five of this book, either for yourself, your acts, or your potential clients.

11. Are you aggressive?
You need chutzpah to be successful in any business. Being aggressive doesn't mean being confrontational or abrasive, but you have to ask for what you want and be relentless in coming up with ways to get it.

12. Are you aligning yourself with the right people?
You will interact with an expansive network of individuals who possess a variety of talents, personalities, and aspirations. Your contacts are a reflection of you; you have to be able to advance your career by interacting with them. Make sure that you are around people who are as positive and creative as you wish to be.

13. *Are you positive?*
You will certainly get back what you give out, so you need to generate positivity in those that you encounter. If you find that your outlook is negative, ascertain why this is and determine what you need to do to change it.

14. *Can you create plans and keep to them until they're completed?*
You need chart a course before you take it. Otherwise, you're just being blown to where the strongest winds may take you. In a music business career, you can't anticipate everything that's going to influence you, but you can plan weekly, monthly, and yearly goals.

15. *Do you listen to and chart trends in music?*
Can you name the top-selling artists of this year? What trends are currently bubbling under the surface that are most likely to become major sources of revenue for record labels this year? Music works on cycles, and what is happening on the top of the charts influences everything else beneath it.

16. *Do you read at least three music industry magazines a week?*
Go to your local library, check out online sources, subscribe to magazines, or stand at the newsstand and read until the proprietor asks you to leave. There is new information every week, and you need to know it.

17. *Do you have access to a music-industry resource library, and do you use it?*
Some local songwriting organizations pool their resources to purchase books and periodicals that the members share. Do you know others who would be interested in sharing materials with you in such a relationship?

18. *Can you work locally?*
Strong grass roots are vital to national movements. Meet your local movers and shakers and begin to use them as resources. Let them know what you do, and create situations to work together. Create a scene.

19. *Are you in the right place geographically?*
You have to go where it is. If you need to live in a major music capitol, don't arrive broke, and do your homework. Don't go to New York to work with country artists, or to Nashville to do hip-hop.

If you've answered negatively to more than four of any of these questions, you may need to reevaluate your commitment to success. Your ambition, energy, and resourcefulness are the tools that will determine your potential. You can certainly change and improve to succeed by establishing your goals, fueling your motivation, and figuring out an angle to position yourself for success.

We've all met people who have told us that they look back with regret that they didn't attempt something they could have accomplished. They will live out the rest of their lives with the uncertainty that maybe, if they'd just tried, they could have been successful at something very special. If you are determined to succeed in the music business, you will find a way to do it.

Networking Resources

The following is a list of noteworthy events at which rabid industry networking is the key activity. You should contact the specific organizations listed for information about their events. You can also check to see if it's possible to trade volunteer time in exchange for admission to events; many need qualified people to staff them.

Some organizations will provide free admissions to groups and publications that assist in promoting their event via print ads in local papers or organization newsletters.

MUSIC INDUSTRY TRADE EVENTS

AES Convention
Audio Engineering Society
60 E. 42nd St.
New York, NY 10165-2520
(212) 661-8528
Annual convention for engineers and audio manufacturers.

Canadian Music Week
5399 Eglinton Ave. W. #310
Toronto, Ontario, Canada M9C5K6
(416) 695-9236
Held in Toronto in mid-March. Participants are selected to perform from demo tapes. Performances are held in concert venues and clubs.

CMJ Music Marathon, Music Fest, Film Fest
11 Middle Neck Rd. Suite 400
Great Neck, NY 11021-2301
(516) 498-3150
www.cmj.com
Fall convention for college and alternative radio with seminars, exhibitions, live showcases, and the CMJ Music Awards, held in New York City.

Emerging Artists & Talent in Music (EAT'M) Conference and Festival
2030 E. Flamingo Rd. #110,
Las Vegas, NV 89119
(792) 792-9430
www.EAT-M.com
A growing music conference that showcases artists and presents well-attended music business seminars. The event is held in spring in Las Vegas and features performers selected from demo tapes.

Folk Alliance Annual Conference
1001 Connecticut Ave. NW #501
Washington, DC 20036
(202) 835-3655
A four-day conference that takes place in mid-February and includes artists, agents, artists, administrators, folks societies, and others. It is held in various locations around the U.S.

Kerrville Folk Festival
P.O. Box 1466
Kerrville, TX 78029
(830) 257-3600
www.kerrville-music.com
A nonprofit event that hosts a three-day songwriters school, a booking and management seminar, and a concert competition. Participants are selected from demos. It is held during the Kerrville Folk Festival in early June.

NAMM (National Association of Music Merchandisers)
(800) 767-NAMM
Both the winter convention in Los Angeles and the summer convention, now held in Nashville, are gigantic conventions. It is the opportunity for manufacturers of the latest musical gear to meet retailers. This event attracts celebrities, occupies literally acres of space, and creates a cacophony that will leave an indelible print on your eardrums. This event is not open to the general public, but the press and reps from retail, wholesale, and audio dealers are welcome, and there are many creative ways to get to attend. It's quite a scene.

North By Northeast Music Festival and Conference (NXNE)
185A Danforth Ave., 2nd Fl.
Toronto, Ontario Canada MK4 IN2
(416) 469-0986
www.nxne.com
An early summer event that takes place at over 20 venues and three outdoor stages in downtown Toronto and features a variety of musical genres. Festival performers are selected from demo tapes and packages. In addition to the live shows, the conference features mentor sessions, panels and workshops

Northern California Songwriters Association Conference
(650) 654-3966 or (800) FOR-SONG
A well-organized conference that features seminar song screening sessions, performances, one-on-one sessions, and concerts. It takes place the second weekend in September at Foothill College in Los Altos Hills and attracts heavy industry participation from Los Angeles and Nashville. Highly recommended.

NSAI Spring Symposium
15 Music Square W,
Nashville, TN 37203
(615) 256-3354
www.nashvillesongwriters.com
An event that takes place in April in Nashville with publisher and pro song evaluations and group sessions. Presented by Nashville Songwriters Association International (NSAI).

South by Southwest
P.O. Box 4999
Austin, Texas 78765
(512) 467-7979
www.sxsw.com/sxsw
Over 800 bands perform in over 40 venues for five wild nights, deep in the heart of Texas. This event includes music business trade/seminars for independent musicians plus mentor sessions and interactive/multimedia festivals held one week before the conference.

We read magazines not only for entertainment, but because they provide a lifeline to the music industry. I recommend the following to help educate you about the business.

American Songwriter
1009-A 17th Ave. S.
Nashville, TN 37212-2201
(615) 321-6096
A rare magazine indeed, one geared for songwriters. Based in Nashville, American Songwriter covers the national music scene admirably in its bimonthly publications. The journalism is concise and relevant, and there are excellent cover stories and special issues. The interviews feature writers from many genres, and the columns cover songwriting activities, not only in Music City, but across the U.S.

Back Stage
1515 Broadway 14th Fl.
New York, NY 10036-8901
(212) 764-7300
www.backstage.com
An East Coast performing artists' trade publication that includes classifieds, industry news, and much more.

Back Stage West
5055 Wilshire Blvd. 6th Fl.
Los Angeles, CA 90036
(800) 437-3183
The West Coast version of this publication, now merged with Dramalogue to form one magazine. It includes casting notices and tech and musicians wanted ads that are generally geared to theatrical and the cinema arts.

The Beat
P.O. Box 65856
Los Angeles, CA 90065
For anyone interested in the exploding global music scene, this visionary publication is a must-read. Covering African, Brazilian, Indian, and reggae music, plus every other applicable world music form, this magazine is fascinating for musicians wanting to touch the deeper wellspring.

Billboard
1515 Broadway, 39th Fl. New York,
NY 10036
(800) 247-2160
www.billboard.com
This is the essential weekly trade journal. Beg or borrow, or better yet, convince your local library to carry this magazine—this is required reading. Current editor Timothy White maintains the integrity of this venerable publication with on-the-money editorials. Read the charts where every type of music, from the Top 200 to hits from Europe and Asia, are represented. All signings and assignments of music industry personnel are listed as well as milestones—births, deaths, weddings, etc. It reports signings and trends and includes feature stories and special issues. This is the storehouse of information you need to access to be in the music business.

Daily Variety
5700 Wilshire Blvd. #120
Los Angeles, CA 90036
(323) 857-6600
A daily entertainment newspaper with music news in addition to extensive reporting on film and television.

Film Music
350 N. Glenoaks Blvd., Suite 201
Burbank, CA 91502
(818) 729-9500, (888) 456-5020
www.filmmusicmag.com
A glossy monthly publication devoted to the art of marrying music with pictures: film, television, multimedia, and beyond. The only magazine of its type in existence, this publication is linked to the Film Music Network with chapters in New York, Los Angeles, and San Francisco. Film Music features interviews with major figures in the composing world, plus music editors, songwriters, publishers, engineers, copyists, technicians, and performing rights experts. If your goal is to place your music on the big—or small—screen, this is your number one resource.

The Gavin Report
140 Second St.
San Francisco, CA 94104
(415) 495-1990
Weekly listing of radio charts. Highly recommended to get a feel for what's going out over the airwaves.

Grammy Magazine
3402 Pico Blvd.
Santa Monica, CA 90405
(310) 392-3777
A new, hip glossy publication published quarterly by the National Academy of Recording Arts and Sciences (NARAS). Full of trends, features, and NARAS news, plus, as the title indicates, info on Grammy nominees and winners.

Guitar Player
20085 Stevens Creek Blvd.
Cupertino, CA 95014
Guitar as big business—a wonderful publication for the six-stringer.

Hits Magazine
15477 Ventura Blvd. Suite 300
Sherman Oaks, CA 91403
(818) 501-7900
An expensive, very insider weekly magazine that has a wonderful sense of humor, resulting in some very entertaining reading. Classic photo captions. Highly recommended for readers who want to see how the record industry views and reports on itself with tongue firmly in cheek.

Music Connection
4731 Laurel Canyon Blvd.
North Hollywood, CA 91607
(818) 755-0101
www.musicconnection.com
This LA-based biweekly covers the Los Angeles scene like nothing else. Informative interviews with key A&R personnel, publishers, musicians, and recording artists. Very hip and not afraid to take chances. Club reviews, demo critiques, and an extensive music marketplace with musicians wanted classifieds make this a must-read for any one living, hoping to live, or submitting material or acts to the music industry based in Los Angeles. Very inside information only available here. Highly recommended for serious professionals.

The Performing Songwriter
6620 McCall Dr.
Longmont, CO 80503
(800) 883-7664
www.performingsongwriter.com
What began as a labor of love is now, clearly, a thriving enterprise. Under the direction of publisher Lydia Hutchinson, this glossy publication has thrived as the *magazine for independent artist/writers. Incisive articles, great tips, and a tremendous heart make this a one-of-a-kind publication. Highly recommended.*

Radio and Records
10100 Santa Monica Blvd. 5th Fl.
Los Angeles, CA 90067-4004
(310) 788-1625
A bible of the radio industry, R&R (as it's known) reports weekly on the latest from the airwaves.

SongLink International
23 Belsize Crescent
London NW3 5QY England
www.songlink.com
As the music business becomes more international, having a trans-Atlantic link is vital. Under the direction of David Stark, this publication features what artists are looking for songs in Europe and beyond and spotlights news and features from the continental music biz.

BOOKS AND DIRECTORIES

I recommend the following publications to track the frenetic movements of the ever-elusive executives who populate our business.

The A&R Registry
Music Attorney Legal & Business Affairs Registry
The Music Publisher Registry
Film & Television Music Guide
All published by SRS Publishing
7510 Sunset Blvd. #1041
Los Angeles, CA 90046-3418
(800) 377-7411

Recording Industry Sourcebook
Intertec Publishing
6400 Hollis Street, Suite 12
Emeryville, CA 94608
510-653-3307

The Yellow Pages of Rock
The Album Network
120 N. Victory Blvd.
Burbank, CA 91502
(818) 944-4000

INDUSTRY ORGANIZATIONS

American Federation of Musicians (AFM)
1501 Broadway, Suite 600
New York, NY 10036
(800) 762-3444

AFM Los Angeles
1777 North Vine Street Suite 500
Hollywood, CA 90028
(323) 461-3441

American Society of Composers, Authors and Publishers
(ASCAP)
One Lincoln Plaza
New York, NY 10023
(212) 621-6000

ASCAP/L.A.
7920 Sunset Blvd. Third Floor
Los Angeles, CA 90046
(323) 883-1000

ASCAP/Nashville
2 Music Square West
Nashville TN 37203
(615) 742-5000

American Society of Music Arrangers and Composers
(ASMAC)
P.O. Box 17840
Encino, CA 91416
(818) 994-4661

Broadcast Music Incorporated (BMI)
320 W. 57th St.
New York, NY 10019
(212) 586-2000

BMI/L.A.
8730 Sunset Blvd.
Los Angeles, CA 90069
(310) 659-9109

BMI/Nashville
10 Music Sq. East
Nashville, TN 37203
(615) 291-6700

The Film Music Network
350 N. Glenoaks Blvd., Suite 201
Burbank, CA 91502
(818) 729-9500, (888) 726-7338

Los Angeles Music Network
P.O Box 8934
Universal City, CA 91618-8934
(818) 769-6095

Los Angeles Women in Music
PO Box 1817 Burbank, CA 91507
(213) 243-6440
www.lawim.org

Nashville Songwriters Association International (NSAI)
1701 West End Ave. 3rd Fl,
Nashville, TN 37203
(615) 256-3354, (800) 321-6008
www.nashvillesongwriters.com.

National Academy of Popular Music (NAPM)
330 W. 58th St. #411
New York, NY 10019-1827
(212) 957-9230

National Academy of Recording Arts & Sciences (NARAS)
3402 Pico Blvd.
Santa Monica, CA 90405
(310) 392-3777

Northern California Songwriters Association (NCSA)
1724 Laurel St. #120
San Carlos, CA 94070
(650) 654-3966

Outmusic
c/o The Center
New York, NY 10011-7799
(212) 330-9197

Recording Musicians Association (RMA)
817 Vine Street, Suite 209
Hollywood, CA 90038
(310) 462-4762

The Society of Composers and Lyricists (SCL)
400 South Beverly Drive Suite 214
Beverly Hills, CA 90212
(310) 281-2812
www: http://www.filmscore.org

Songwriters Guild of America (SGA)/East Coast
1500 Harbor Blvd.
Weehawken, NJ 07097-6732
(201) 867-7603

SGA/Los Angeles
6430 Sunset Boulevard #705
Hollywood, CA 90028
(323) 462-1108

SGA/Nashville
1222 16th Avenue South, Suite 25
Nashville, TN 37212
(615-329-1782)

SESAC, Inc.
421 W. 54th St.
New York, NY 10019
(212) 586-3450

SESAC/Nashville
55 Music Square E.
Nashville, TN 37203
(615) 320-0055

Women in Music
P.O Box 441
Radio City Station
New York, NY 10101
(212) 459-4580